Passages of Time

Passages of Time

Creative Writing from the Cheshire Prize for Literature 2023

Edited by
Harry Parkin, Lucy Andrew,
Matt Davies and Sally West

University of Chester Press

First published 2024
by University of Chester Press
Parkgate Road
Chester CH1 4BJ

Printed and bound in the UK by the
LIS Print Unit
University of Chester
Cover designed by the LIS Graphics Team
University of Chester

This collection © University of Chester, 2024
Individual contributions © their respective authors

The moral rights of Harry Parkin, Lucy Andrew, Matt Davies and Sally West to be identified as the joint editors of this work have been asserted in accordance with the Copyright, Designs and Patents Act 1988

The moral rights of the contributors to be identified as the authors of this work have been asserted in accordance with the Copyright, Designs and Patents Act 1988

All Rights Reserved
No part of this publication may be reproduced, stored in a retrieval system or transmitted in any form or by any means without the prior permission of the copyright owner, other than as permitted by UK copyright legislation or under the terms and conditions of a recognised copyright licensing scheme

A catalogue record of this book is available
from the British Library

ISBN 978-1-910481-31-8

CONTENTS

Contributors	ix
Foreword **Livi Michael**	xix
Preface **Harry Parkin**	xxi

Primary Poems

Talking to My Dad **Isabel Airosa**	1
This Year **Eilidh Whelan**	2
Breaking Free **Esme Alice Blue**	4

Primary Stories

The Life of a Different Mind **Nadia Kazem**	6
The Sea of Tranquility 2132 **Jack Waring**	11
Dogs to the Rescue **Lucy Copping**	16

Passages of Time

SECONDARY POETRY

Electric Boots — 20
Lottie Hughes

Flight — 21
Martha Blue

SECONDARY STORIES

A Homage to Home: Exploring loss — 23
of identity due to the immigrant experience,
from Malaysia to the UK
Aisya Imya

The Price — 27
Patrick Gambles

The Killer Punchline — 31
Flynn Alexander Hampson

CHILDREN'S LITERATURE

Stars Come Out — 36
Glyn Matthews

The Ballad — 42
Jo Winchcombe

Baby it is OK to be. OK — 48
Sarah O'Hanlon

Contents

POETRY

Unconditional **Joanne Lacey**	50
Sticking Place **Helen Kay**	52
Reunion **David Percy**	53
In Which I Discuss the Notion of Happiness with Raymond Carver **Angi Holden**	54
Tribe **Joy Winkler**	57
Lasagne for Breakfast **David Horner**	58

SHORT STORIES

Bernard Can Sing **Rob Bisset**	59
The Sailor's Vault **RD Kay**	64
Return Date **Keith Murray**	70

Passages of Time

Differential Diagnosis   75
Andi Courtland

The Keepers of Shells   80
Nina Patterson

The Sound of No Door Slamming   85
John Paul Davies

SCRIPTWRITING

Phantom Life   91
Helen East

Bed   97
Meryl Walker

Jonah   109
Patrick Smythe

CONTRIBUTORS

Isabel Airosa who is 10 years old, is half English and half Portuguese, living in Wirral. She has a cracking sense of humour, and is currently in her own Swiftie Era! She enjoys reading all sorts of books, baking delicious cakes, lambing every Easter, and observing the night sky with her Papa.

Rob Bisset is a 68-year-old pensioner with 11 years of experience as a writer. He was born in Hartlepool and thus is technically a 'monkey hanger' but from four to 17 years of age he lived in Bolton and then moved to London for five years. Since 1980 he has been resident in Cheshire commuting to work each day in Manchester until taking early retirement in 2013. After a lifetime of writing factual reports he turned to writing short stories on retirement. The transition has been difficult as scientific reports must 'mean what they say and say what they mean' without the risk of ambiguity, whilst modern fiction tries to paint a picture that each reader may see differently. Other hobbies include cycling with other old men (none of them wears Lycra), photography, playing dominoes in the Mobberley and Knutsford league and most importantly caring for grandchildren.

Esme Alice Blue lives in Cheshire. She enjoys writing poetry and haikus about nature, horses and humorous things. She likes to mountaineer in Scotland, Ireland, Wales and the English Lake District, is learning to play the piano and enjoys photography. Most of all she enjoys meeting with her friends. Esme co-writes *The Outlaw*, the literary magazine for Junior Members of The Arthur Ransome Society, alongside her sisters.

Passages of Time

Esme's achievements include first prize in poetry competitions held by RSPB Wildverse, Oxford Festival of Science and Ideas, East Riding Poetry Festival, Elmbridge Festival and Writing East Midlands/Derbyshire. She has also had many haiku poems published by the Japan Society. Thanks again to the Cheshire Prize judges for appreciating her writing.

Martha Blue lives in Cheshire and her poetry often has an environmental focus; she enjoys being outdoors and is an enthusiastic Junior Ranger for a National Park Authority – a wild life is a happier life! She enjoys listening to classical music and plays violin in a youth orchestra. She also creates botanical art cards. Martha appreciates reading the poetry of Ted Hughes (having won the Ted Hughes Elmet Trust Poetry Prize in 2018) and Christina Rosetti and the work of the Brontës. Other successes include winning first prize at the Elmbridge Festival, Write Out Loud, the Solstice Prize (East Midlands) and the Causley Trust, while her poetry has been published in collections such as *HEBE* magazine and the Stratford Felix Dennis Literature Festival anthology. Martha has come close to winning the Cheshire Prize previously and so is delighted to have done so on this occasion.

Lucy Copping is eight years old and goes to Tushingham-with-Grindley CE Primary School. She loves writing at school and in her spare time too. Lucy also enjoys drama and dance and attends Stagecoach in Chester. She loves animals and has two dogs, Cooper and Huxley, who inspired her story, 'Dogs to the Rescue'.

Contributors

Andi Courtland hails from Middlewich and spent his early life in Cheshire before peregrinations elsewhere. An early experience with medical counselling and its challenges led Andi to become involved in communications skills training for medical professionals, an involvement that continues to this day. This may or may not have inspired the story included in this anthology, though no representation of any person, living or dead, is intended or should be inferred ...!

John Paul Davies was born in Birkenhead, and has lived in Navan, Ireland since 2013. A former winner of the RTÉ Guide/Penguin Ireland Short Story Award, and the Letheon Poetry Prize, he has been placed in competitions such as the Waterford Poetry Prize, the TU Dublin Story Prize, and the Cheshire Prize for Literature. John's stories and poems appear in journals including *Southword: New International Writing*, *Stand*, *Vastarien: A Literary Journal*, *Banshee*, *Channel*, *Crannóg Magazine*, *The Manchester Review*, *The Maine Review*, *Apex Magazine*, *PseudoPod* and *Alfred Hitchcock's Mystery Magazine*. A poem of his hangs in the finest pub in Liverpool, The Ship & Mitre.

Helen East grew up in Dr Barnardo's Boughton Hall Children's Home in Chester where she was regularly told off for telling stories. Today, most of Helen's stories have been both short- and longlisted in writing competitions for the theatre, television and radio.

Passages of Time

Patrick Gambles is a student at St Anselm's College in Birkenhead and is looking to be a writer in the future. He has performed with Simon Armitage on his library tour of the UK and has also worked with Canadian and Australian writers in the 3UP course to draft plays for the University of Toronto. Equally, he has written plays with Theatre Porto to tour around primary schools in the local area and was formerly a member of their Young Writers group. Additionally, he has been shortlisted for both the 'Frank Moran' and 'Young Writers Through Their Eyes' competitions as well as writing the short film the 'Oracle' with the British Film Institute. He would like to thank the University of Chester for publishing his story.

Flynn Alexander Hampson is 12 years old and has loved writing from the day he started school. He loves everything about history, politics and *The Big Bang Theory* and plays rugby in his free time. When Flynn grows up, he hopes to write historical fiction and become a Time Lord.

Angi Holden is a retired lecturer, whose published writing includes prize-winning poetry, short stories and flash fiction. Her current work explores differing perspectives of family and identity. She has been writing most of her life, most recently at a desk so covered in leaves, feathers and shells collected by her grandchildren that it resembles a nature table.

David Horner worked as a freelance writer in schools and libraries for over 20 years in the UK and abroad, publishing 10 books of poems for children. Between 2019 and 2022 he had three books on creative writing in schools published by

Contributors

Brilliant Publications. In the past he has had poems published in magazines including *Critical Quarterly* and *The Spectator* and featured on Radio 4's *Pick of the Week*, and more recently in *The Cannon's Mouth*. With his good friend Michael Jackson (no, not that one) he writes resources for classroom use in the UK and the US. They work under the name Goodeyedeers and all the money raised goes to their chosen charity, Medequip4kids.

Lottie Hughes is a sixth former from Chester. She is obsessed with Jane Austen, her cat, and wearing copious amounts of eyeliner. She won first prize in Shepton Mallet's Festival Poetry Competition and was highly commended in Waltham Forest's Poetry Competition.

Aisya Imya, more commonly known as Ash, is an 18-year-old author from Chester. She was born in Malaysia, and has lived in Birmingham, Nottingham and Manchester whilst growing up. Ash enjoys crocheting, films and art; and the stories she has written surround her personal experience of immigration from Malaysia to the UK. She hopes to share more of these stories as she continues to her Art History and English Literature degree at university.

Helen Kay is a Dabber (Nantwich born and still there). Her second pamphlet, *This Lexia & Other Languages* (v.press) arrived in 2020. She curates an online platform for dyslexic poets: Poetry Dyslexia and Imagination. She was the winner of the 2023 Ironbridge and Repton Prizes and the Dithering Chaps pamphlet *Competition* in 2024.

Passages of Time

RD Kay has lived in lots of different places over the years but has decided Chester is the best. She runs all her plotlines past her dog first – the best way to get unqualified approval.

Nadia Kazem is nine. She has lived all of her life in Delamere in Cheshire and attends school there. She loves writing stories and being creative. She also loves animals – especially polar bears – and wants to be a zoologist when she grows up. Aside from writing, her other hobbies include music – she plays the keyboard and clarinet – and skiing.

Joanne Lacey is a new writer who currently lives in Liverpool. She works as a psychotherapist and a social researcher. Joanne is intrigued by people, how they feel, think, and experience the world. She is enjoying using poetry to explore and express different human experiences.

Glyn Matthews is an escaped teacher of expressive arts and ex-professional artist from Congleton, Cheshire, with a passion for shorter written forms. He delves into 'inner space' to discover interesting characters that populate his stories. His story for children, 'Stars Come Out', winner of the Cheshire Prize for Literature was written not just for children but for the child within us all.

Keith Murray was born in Liverpool and educated in Cheshire. His interests include theatre, opera and travel, as well as searching for new sources of creative inspiration. These can usually be found in the least expected places.

Contributors

Sarah O'Hanlon grew up in Chester and currently lives in Kingston upon Thames. She has always loved poetry and is an advocate of writing for wellbeing. She is trained in creative writing for therapeutic purposes and alongside her job working with care leavers, she facilitates writing workshops and courses to various groups in her local community. She has a beautiful one-year-old who is helping her to look with new curiosity at all aspects of the world and life and is an inspiration for a lot of fun new writing.

Nina Patterson has always been an avid reader and loves stories that are unpredictable, psychologically compelling, mystical or a little off kilter! She spent her childhood overseas before returning to her native Scotland to study Psychology at the University of Edinburgh. Nina currently lives in Chester with her husband and two teenage children and is a Senior Lecturer in Mental Health and Wellbeing at Wrexham University. A number of her short stories, including 'The Keepers of Shells', draw inspiration from the rugged landscape and seas surrounding the Shetland Islands where her parents still live.

David Percy moved to Chester with his wife and family in 1986 after he had joined Liverpool City Council as a Principal Landscape Architect. He worked on urban regeneration, playground and urban countryside schemes for 16 years, before being appointed Tree and Landscape Officer at Conwy County Borough Council, where he extended his career beyond retirement age because he liked the job so much. He enjoys gardening, spending time with his two granddaughters, reading and occasionally trying to write poetry.

Passages of Time

Patrick (Pat) Smythe – who has nothing to do with the once famous British show jumper after whom he was inadvertently named – is highly flattered and encouraged to be receiving his first publication courtesy of the University of Chester, himself having avoided tertiary education. A Cheshire Ulsterman, he has thus far maintained a near-Trappist silence about his literary aspirations, though that may be about to change! Hobbies include rock-climbing, bridge, arguing with *Question Time* audiences and (when time allows) propping up the bars of Irish centres from Leeds to London.

Meryl Walker lives part of the time in Neston and that's the part of the time she likes best! She's written short and long plays, and while she's been lucky enough to have many of them performed she's never been published before! When not writing she's usually fighting either procrastination or insomnia – which is what inspired 'Bed'.

Jack Waring is 11 years old and lives in East Cheshire. He recently completed his very happy time at High Legh Primary School and now attends Lymm High School. Jack has always loved writing and creating characters. He loves reading and his favourite authors are JRR Tolkien, Alan Garner and Anthony Horowitz. Jack also loves sport and plays football and tennis in Lymm. He has very much enjoyed writing the story for the Cheshire Prize for Literature and hopes to continue writing short stories during his new chapter at high school.

Contributors

Eilidh Whelan lives in a small village approximately 12 miles from Chester. She entered her final year of primary school in September 2024. She has always enjoyed reading and writing. After her mother became very sick during 2023, Eilidh turned to her writing to help her express her emotions. This is when her poem, 'This Year' was created. Though still incredibly modest about it, she is thrilled to have won such a prestigious prize and feels 'quite proud' of herself. As well as writing, Eilidh loves to draw, spend time with her family and her younger sister, Elsie, her best friend, Nell and her cats. On top of all of this, she occasionally likes to partake in the odd thrill-seeking activity, much to her mother's dismay! Next year she hopes to try out the giant zip line at Zip World in Conwy, finally being old enough to give it a try! Eilidh would like to again thank all of the judges who chose her poem as the winning entry in the primary poetry category, as well as extending her thanks to all those involved in organising such a fantastic competition.

Jo Winchcombe currently works as an Assistant Academic Librarian, at the University of Chester. Prior to this, she was a primary school teacher at various schools on the Wirral and in Cheshire. In 2007 she completed an MA in Critical and Creative Writing at the University and, during that time, her short story, 'Read Me', was published in the University's in-house creative writing magazine, *Pandora's Box*. Three years later, in 2010, she was delighted to have her story 'The Rescue', published online, as part of a regional flash fiction competition. After taking an extended break from writing, to look after her young daughter, she submitted a piece of young adult fiction, 'Not in the Hands of Boys', to the Cheshire Prize for Literature in 2017. She was subsequently shortlisted and published in that year's anthology, *Opening Words*. Jo is passionate about writing, particularly within the YA genre and is absolutely thrilled to be part of the forthcoming anthology.

Joy Winkler is a former Cheshire Poet Laureate and author of several poetry collections, a verse/drama called 'TOWN', an acclaimed toured piece for theatre called 'Lightning under their Skirts' and a novel called *Morgan*. She has worked as a facilitator of creative writing in many community settings including HMP Styal, Writing Lives in Salford and for Cartwheel Arts and is the founder member of Macclesfield Creative Writers. Currently she holds the post of Writer in Residence at RHS Tatton in Cheshire where she also facilitates regular workshops.

FOREWORD

It was a great honour to be invited to the awards ceremony for the Cheshire Prize, which is unique in giving prizes in so many categories. The evening itself was a delight – a celebration of talent in all the different genres of writing, poetry, fiction, children's fiction, drama. And what a wonderful way to commemorate this award – by producing this beautiful book!

It's so exciting to see your own work in print and to have something to treasure. Anthologies used to be called 'treasuries' and I rather like that word. It conveys the sense of something precious, and varied, where wealth is stored. And this anthology is exactly that.

There are many reasons why it's good to be published in an anthology. It establishes a connection with the other writers in it that wouldn't otherwise exist. It is a calling card for those of you who go on to pursue a career in writing – to be mentioned on your writing CV. And even if you don't want to be a professional writer, it is still something to treasure (there's that word again) – a reminder that someone recognised the talent you have.

All the contributors should be thanked for making this book so fantastic. But also, we should not forget the dedication of those who worked behind the scenes to make it possible. A book is one of the most remarkable things human civilisation has ever produced, and the work involved is considerable. It requires time, patience, judgement, and skill. So, a huge thank you to everyone who contributed to this particular book in any way – by writing, judging, editing, or designing it. And congratulations on producing something so uniquely valuable.

Passages of Time

Perhaps its most important value is that it will go out into the world, to encourage and inspire anyone who reads it. The effects of good writing are immeasurable and often invisible. Each time you give the gift of your words to the world, you change it a little bit.

So may this anthology travel far and well, and light the flame of inspiration wherever it goes!

Livi Michael
Award-winning novelist, children's author and podcaster about the short story form

PREFACE

Time affects us all. It has an impact on our lives every day. Sometimes this impact is trivial, and sometimes it is life changing. Sometimes time waits for no one, and sometimes it seems to stop. As it passes, it allows life to grow and death to take hold. It allows relationships to build and friendships to fall apart. It can heal and it can hurt. It is good and bad. It is contradictory and confused. It is so significant and ever-present, yet at the same time mysterious and incomprehensible, that a collective desire to process and understand it and its effects is no great surprise. Such a desire is reflected in this collection of writing. The subject of time is woven into the pages that follow, represented in poetry, short stories, children's literature, and scripts.

The topics may be different: in the short stories, we see visions of the future, a hope of new beginnings, time's effect on relationships, and a race against time to catch a killer; in the children's literature, we see a celebration of childhood, a new relationship change as day turns to night, and characters waiting for love in a tale of a past time; in the poetry we see efforts to process and reflect on love, grief, coming of age, and ageing; in the scripts we see the impact of new life, the comedic absurdity of monotony and repetition, and a worrying glimpse of things to come. But time unites them all, bringing them together in a representation of how time had, has, and will continue to have a hold on us all.

Passages of Time

We invite you to read on, exploring the kinds of experiences and emotions that shape our lives as you wander through these passages of time.

Dr Harry Parkin
Senior Lecturer in English Language
Programme Leader, MRes Storytelling
School for the Creative Industries

Primary Poems

TALKING TO MY DAD

Isabel Airosa

The sun shone down from the sky,
I said to my Dad, 'Tell me why!'
To my utter confusion,
He said, 'Gas, nebula, fusion.'
'That's helpful,' I said with a sigh.

THIS YEAR

Eilidh Whelan

This year started out quite bad,
I was worried and fairly sad.
My mum got sick,
And I wished I could flick
A magic wand to make her better.

When she was away,
I felt scared but couldn't say,
I just really missed her and wanted a cuddle,
It was a horrible feeling knowing she was in trouble,
And there was nothing I could do to help.

The day she came home I was super excited,
My whole family too were extremely delighted.
It was hard at first to see her struggle and in pain,
But each day I saw her strength regain,
And life gradually became a lot better.

Then after a while she took a turn for the worse,
And she went back to the hospital to see the doctors and nurse.
This time I was truly terrified she might die,
But she fought for her life not ready to say goodbye,
And she came back to us.

This Year

I love my mum and I'm so incredibly proud,
So I've written this poem to tell this crowd.
I think she is really brave and I feel very lucky,
We've since had some amazing adventures – the rest of the year has been less sucky.
Thank goodness for that!

So this poem is for you mum,
For everything that you have overcome.
You simply are the best mum EVER!
This next line I mean always and forever.
I love you infinitely!

BREAKING FREE

Esme Alice Blue

Heaving up a not-really rocky slope,
    itself hidden within a deciduous coniferous
       pine forest, this gritty path is speckled with miniature,
      dark froglets
all vaulting, exploding, springing, hurdling to their
  sheltered pond.
      And so here there is this deep, dark, musty forest, beside
           its stony, old path full of secrets.

Here, where once bears and wolves leapt out
from behind every bush and tree,
shadows
blend in beautifully with the sun-dapply leaves, and thick,
  ancient
boughs of pines and firs.

        Once spat out of the maw of forest, I bound
          across curlew-moorland
and a world of dew, and soaked, soak up another
                  slope to the top, where
    lies a flattened summit, flat as a table,
stone-slabbed and grand-blocked, and then my kite.
          I cast it into the sharp, piercing-cold air.

Breaking Free

As it hovers, flaps, then soars, it swoops higher and farther
away as I pay out yards of cord behind it.
Imagine it somersaulting! In the thinned icy air above the
  snow-blanketed
fields and moors, on a crisp, blue-skied day,
            I walk slowly downhill, with my kite flying out
                wildly about me.

In a frozen sudden, the kite tugs away, sailing out freely
  across the innocent moors.
                It heads towards the forest. I crash after it,
        clambering over a crumbling stone wall,
through clingy bracken and mossy heathers.
The cord tangles in a fingery yearling fir tree.
            I can finally catch up with it, unwind it from the
                tree, and wind it up.
                    The kite seems alive, wanting to fly free
                    up and up. The sun sets as I meander
                    back through the deep,
                    dark forest. But I have my kite!

Primary Stories

THE LIFE OF A DIFFERENT MIND

Nadia Kazem

This might surprise you, but I am a squirrel and you, yes, you, have found my very own diary. You have got to take care of this book because it has my life in it; well, not literally but metaphorically, so get ready to not only read but feel and be in a squirrel's life …

Dear diary, today is a BIG day for me because I am currently writing to you on my birthday. Even though I don't know what age I am turning, I am still enthusiastic. First for breakfast, I had nuts and I will tell you one thing, nuts make me absolutely NUTS. I dug into my cashews, pecans, pistachios, peanuts and so on. It was like the best type of salad you could imagine, but instead of those vegetables there were nuts and nuts and nuts … oops, I think I'm starting to go nuts! Oh sorry, how many times have I said nuts? OH, I did it again! OK, let's just get off the topic of breakfast.

Next, I went climbing in the trees of a woodland and, oh, how calm it was. Personally, I think it was as calm as you in your bedroom with your door closed writing in your diary, and you can tell that I just thought of this simile right now. But trust me it is pretty calm, despite the fact I can hear people wandering round my house which is a tree and the fact that my brother is playing extremely loudly, but despite that pretty calm. However, back to my birthday. When we were climbing in the massive dreamland of oak and birch and a

The Life of a Different Mind

touch of ash, I stumbled across a being. A rather big being, I should say, with massive legs, tree-trunk arms and a huge face. So many thoughts were racing through my mind: Who was this monster? Have I ever seen a thing like this? Until one special thought stumbled upon me – it was a human! With its distinctive face, you can't miss an animal like that. Oh, and if you are a human no offence, but you guys stink, unlike us squirrels who are clean and have a smell of fresh walnuts.

Anyways, back to my birthday. One of these human beings thought that I apparently was 'cute', and so they said 'I am going to make this lil' guy my very own pet' with an ending of 'awwww'. So with those little-girl words she picked me up (in a rather uncomfortable way) and brought me to what she called 'home'.

It may have been home to her, but to me it was just one big block of concrete with glass squares in it and a roof chucked on. What I call home is a hole in a tree. After a long walk (for her because she was picking me up like a lovely, innocent puppy when I am actually a wild, vicious squirrel) we finally reached 'home'. There was already a squirrel enclosure there just for me, and also a PINK collar with the name Mr McFluffy Pants written on it.

I didn't want to put the collar on and turn into Mr McFluffy Pants, but luckily enough, you know how this is happening in England (well you didn't, but now you do), and the thing is that in England you can't keep a squirrel in the house, so they either had to kill me or let me be FREE, and drum roll please ………. they KILLED me! No, just kidding, they let me go, but the bad thing was that they kept the collar on me, so when they went in the woods and saw a giant shiny pink glare in their eyes they knew it was certainly me.

Passages of Time

Right, now you may be thinking 'Oh well the story is finished', but it's only halfway through, so just go and have your lunch and I will go have mine, and then you can read some more.

Written by Mr McFluffy Pants.
(Not really my name, but that's what the collar says.)

OK, it's one lunch later and you are ready right? I said RIGHT? Okay good. Now time for our next tale, so sit down on your favourite beanbag chair or get settled where your teenage siblings always watch their horror films and Ready, Set, READ!

Dear diary, today is another BORING school day and I almost want to change the font of my writing because right now I am the opposite of excited. No, not that, I am the opposite of super-duper extra quadruple excited and if you don't know how NOT excited I am here is how not excited I feel. Imagine you, YES you, have some homework to do. I am not talking about a tiny little test or two, I am talking about like six weeks' worth of homework and you only have less than 24 hours to do it because it is ALL due TOMORROW, and you are all sweaty and hot and nervous and SOOOOO not excited! Well, that, my dear, is how not excited I am for school.

Anyways, let's get back to school, no sorry, the story/ my diary entry. As you know, I was not excited so tried to persuade my mum and dad to not take me to school, but eventually they made me go.

At school, it was the same boring stuff like nut maths and squirrel science, but there was a twist. At lunchtime (yes, whilst I was eating my cashew and peanut butter sandwich), a boy, or should I say a squirrel screamed, 'FOOD FIGHT!',

The Life of a Different Mind

and once I heard the word 'fight' I was off running out of the cafeteria, trying not to let one nut scrape against my fluffy fur.

After what seemed like an obstacle course, I finally got out of the hall breathing like I had just jumped off a 50-metre platform with no harness on. After school had ended, I found out that Jock-Jack the school bully had demanded 'Gimme Your Lunch Money' of a squirrel called Peter who said, if Jock-Jack didn't take his lunch money he would shout 'Food fight,' and everybody would fight and slowly a riot would form. Because of the use of the word riot in Peter's sentence, Jock-Jack said 'deal.'

But here's the bad news. My mum and dad thought that I had shouted the petrifying words 'FOOD FIGHT' at the whole school, because on the school newspaper there was a picture of me blocking the doors with my arms and breathing so hard that my tummy looked like wobbling jelly! And after I explained the whole story, they found out that it actually wasn't me, but I was still grounded.

Dear diary, another day another strange thing that happened ... I woke up as usual and slipped on my slippers and had nut-cakes (pancakes but with an overflowing amount of nuts, a special treat for me). Next, I went for a morning stroll in the woods, trying to avoid massive human feet when, SMACK, I ran straight into a ball, a very shiny ball indeed. Then the ball moved giving me a sudden fright, but it was only the wind. I grabbed the ball to hold it still. Just when my heart had settled, footsteps came behind me. It was a human child. His hands reached down for the ball picking it – and me – up.

I have no idea how that child didn't notice me, but he didn't, and he kept walking until he reached a nearby playground. There he started throwing the ball up in the air

Passages of Time

with me clinging on to it. I was having the opposite of a good time, feeling like a tennis ball might feel, thinking all the time the child would notice me. But he didn't! He got bored of throwing the ball, and put it on the ground and went to kick it – and me – like a football.

'HEY!' I shouted, except it came out like a squeak.

The boy looked down, surprised.

'Hey,' I tried again, less squeaky.

'You're a squirrel!' the boy said amazed. 'And you can talk!'

'Yeah, duh,' I said, but then I realised I had never talked to a human before.

'What's your name?' the boy asked. 'Mr McFluffy Pants,' I almost answered, but then I realised that wasn't really my name.

'Lloyd,' I said, 'my name is Lloyd.'

'Hi,' the boy said. 'I'm Tom. Can we be friends?'

I thought about my friends at school who got me into trouble starting a food fight and the other human who tried to take me home as a pet. Maybe I was better off on my own. But maybe this boy was different. He looked nice and he looked really hopeful asking me to be his friend.

'OK,' I said.

And that, diary, is how a boy called Tom became best friends with a squirrel!

THE END

THE SEA OF TRANQUILITY 2132

Jack Waring

My name is Adam.
There are flashing lights, beeps, voices whirring around my head. I open my eyes. Around me, people gather, speaking into microphones, rushing about, writing things down. I'm in a clear glass box, wires wrapped around me like cobwebs. I know why they are all here – all these people. I am a miracle. I'm the very first human to be born on the moon.

I put my tiny hands up in front of me. They are normal, 10 perfect pink fingers topped with 10 tiny nails. I wail and cry and feel hunger the same as any baby. My features are those of any human – nothing odd to see here.

Soon, I am removed from my box. For the first time, I breathe in fresh air. I know it's ventilated, but it's still fresh. And incredibly tasty. Seven weeks later, I am living in our 'moon bubble' – that is what the people call it. A wonderful biosphere of filtered air and artificial light that supports our extraordinary community. I am being cared for by this kind woman called Helen. Helen is one of the scientists, always wearing her neat white coat, hair tied back, serious, and professional but with a warm friendly face. I have no parents, I was created in the laboratory, my life started in a petri dish under microscopes, and I developed in an artificial womb.

I wasn't the first – they started with chickens and mice and there's also a pig here somewhere. Helen and the other scientists look after me, but I am aware that I am also their most prized research experiment. I am connected to monitors – they record my breathing, sleeping, heart rate, blood samples, measure my intake and waste. Everything I do is watched and studied.

Then suddenly, a little less attention. Mr Greg, the Chief NASA Scientist, and his team are now focused on the next baby from the lab. She is born nearly three months after me, created the same way and we are siblings.

They have named us two Adam and Eve, and we are the very first human Moonlings. We bond instantly, my sister and I.

I have round-the-clock company and life is good. Helen keeps a close eye on us both and we are allowed to play together. Alongside the scientists, there are robots who help us with chores and teach us. My robot teacher is named Beep and it taught me my first word. There was great excitement when I first spoke and took my first steps. All recorded.

I am growing older, and Beep takes me to see this beautiful blue planet. I gaze at it from the viewing deck in the moon biosphere. Beep tells me that this is Earth and all human life until I was born started there. Down the telescope I can see such detail – other stars, moons, planets; but Earth looks the loveliest. Beep teaches me how hard it is to maintain life on the moon, so I finally understand why I live in a bubble and am only allowed outside if I wear a special suit. Beep tells me that our bubble on the moon is the greatest human achievement and in the 20 years that scientists have spent studying and living here, I am the greatest creation they had made. Apparently, I am totally famous on Earth!

The most heart-rending moment of my life so far is when Helen had to leave a week before my fourth birthday to go back to her family on Earth. She was the first person who had ever held me and kissed me and showed me real human love. It was hard saying goodbye to my first moon mother. She

The Sea of Tranquility 2132

cried too but she explained that she has family on Earth and she misses them.

I am constantly being filmed and photographed. They tell me that everyone on Earth is fascinated with Eve and I and, on the plus side, we get sent lots of gifts. The Earth-humans seem to want photos of me in Nike socks and Disney jumpers; Eve has a 'Barbie' T-shirt. The scientists encourage this. I think it helps them make money. All items from Earth have to be quarantined before we can touch them or play with them.

Lovely Helen left me a Star Wars Lego set. No germs there.

They have started preparing Eve and I for something big – we are going on a journey to Earth. They need to see if we can live like normal humans. The experiments will intensify and we are both scared. Beep will travel with us, keep us company and help us in every way it can. We are going to live in Green City, one of the biggest cities in that world. I've been learning about how to socialise with people on Earth, about school and playtimes and friends and family. I wish we had family waiting to greet us, but I am ready to go to where I should belong. We enter the rocket and begin our journey. It is noisy and cramped in the rocket. Our spacesuits and helmets are heavy, but we have had a lifetime to get used to such clothing.

We are nearing Earth. It looks absolutely astonishing. Such colour – so different from home! The noise intensifies and the rocket shudders and jolts as we enter Earth's atmosphere and prepare to land.

It is all so different here. The air stinks and it is so hot. There are so many people and Eve and I have to wear clothing to protect us from the UV light, heat and our fellow humans. They carry diseases which we have never encountered. The

Passages of Time

doctors have vaccinated us and done all they can to keep us healthy. The rest is up to us and our little bodies.

Planet Earth has three continents – Asia–Africa, America and Eurasia. Green City itself is in Eurasia and is the largest city of the continent with a population of 100 million. All the people have to cover themselves when outside to protect their skin and eyes. The humans live indoors as much as possible and there are undercover tunnels to allow them to move about. The heat here, compared to my climate-controlled home, is unbearable.

Helen came to visit us. We are so happy to see each other again and she brought us presents and photographs of her family. After a short while, though, Helen seems worried and preoccupied. She and Mr Greg talk a lot together, hushed voices. Apparently, we are starting to cause concern. Both Eve and I have developed rashes on our skin. We ache – there is pain in my back and my joints. I don't seem to be able to move about as easily as I could. I sleep more and have to use medicine to help me breathe. The scientists are testing us all the time. I have a tube in my arm for them to do daily blood checks. They are sure that we cannot mix with other children now. There are lots of meetings and discussions, anxious faces.

Any dreams I have about what my life would be like here on Earth are disappearing. I don't think I will have a gang of friends, trips to the beach and the ability to play sport. The books I read are not about a kid like me.

When I sleep, I look out at my moon. Tonight it is full, glowing silver-white and I feel so sad. I don't belong here. I want to go back. I know this is not what they had hoped for. The dream is that we can be interchangeable. The experiment that is us is failing. The risk to our continued life means that

The Sea of Tranquility 2132

we are to be returned back to the moon, to live out our time there, however long we have.

I have such a mix of emotions as Eve and I are placed back on that spaceship back to the moon. We still have Beep and we have each other. Helen is not coming. There are a new bunch of scientists travelling with us – all our faces hidden behind visors and space suits. Beep has promised us that they plan to make us a puppy when we get back. There won't be any more children for a while.

I am happy.
I am going home.

DOGS TO THE RESCUE

Lucy Copping

Once upon a time there were six bad guys and they lived in a cottage in the woods. Their names were Barry, Bingo, Bongo, Billy, Bobby and Berty.

One beautiful evening the bad guys were out prowling the neighbourhood when Bobby whispered in excitement, 'Let's go and break into that house. I heard they are rich,' as he pointed his finger at the lovely looking house. Billy replied, 'Even better – I heard they are on holiday as well, Bobby!' They both agreed they should sneak in – so off they went.

They arrived at the house but there was a problem. A HUGE problem! They opened the door but there was a big sheet of strong metal blocking the doorway so they couldn't get in. But that wouldn't stop them. Bobby had an idea! He went to the garage to get a chainsaw while Billy contacted Barry and Bingo and yelled, 'Get over here quickly! We need your help!'

While Barry and Bingo were making their way over to the house, Bobby found a chainsaw at the back of the garage under an old rusty box. He set the chainsaw into action, and in no time at all, they were in. But that was only the start …

As soon as they set foot in the door, they each felt something spiky beneath their feet. Bobby shouted 'OWWWWWWW!' and Billy cried 'OUCHEEEEEEEE!' Each of them realised they were standing on hundreds of nails! They were jumping and hopping to get out of the patch of nails as fast as they could. They made their way to the room where the safe was kept and opened the door …

Dogs to the Rescue

Suddenly a big punch arm came out and punched Bobby straight in the face! Bobby moaned and groaned and then fell backwards and passed out. Billy went up the stairs, but he was holding on to the banisters. Frantically, Billy bounced down the stairs as the banisters shattered into tiny pieces. Billy screamed into the walkie-talkie, 'We need help. We are at 26 Longwood Avenue. Come now!'

Barry and Bingo sprinted over to Longwood Avenue as fast as their feet would carry them. They entered the house through the back door, thinking they were being smart and avoiding the sharp, spiky nails. Instead, they were met by a slippery oil slick! Before they could stop themselves, they were slipping and sliding all over the place and soon found themselves in a sticky heap on the floor! They slid on their bottoms back towards the door to make a quick exit.

Out they flopped into the back garden, thinking they would get their breath back. But oh no! They looked up to see eight pairs of eyes staring back at them. Yikes! The eyes belonged to four very fluffy but smart dogs. They were also each armed with a Nerf gun! They took one look at the baddies and took aim, hitting them with a barrage of foam bullets, right between the eyes. Barry and Bingo disappeared up the garden path screeching for dear life. The dogs knew that they would not be coming back for a long, long time!

Meanwhile, Bongo and Berty were wandering along the path that Barry and Bingo had disappeared up, not knowing what was waiting for them. As they entered the garden, a long, bendy hose pipe turned on and they were soaked from head to toe. They entered the beautiful house and rapidly they slid this way and that on the slippery floor. They then found a staircase and tiptoed up it quietly, where they saw

Passages of Time

a bedroom, so they went inside. What they didn't realise is that while they were sliding around downstairs, the dogs that live in the house had scattered Lego all over the bedroom floor. Bongo and Berty took one step inside the bedroom and 'OWWWWWWWWWW MY FEET Bongo it's Lego!!' screamed Bertie. 'My poor foot,' cried Bongo as he hopped onto the bed.

The bad guys had had enough of this crazy house and all its slippery, spiky traps. They had to get out that minute. So, they all made their way slowly down to the living room, being careful to avoid Lego, oil, the collapsed banister, the punch arm and the nails all over the floor. Then they sat down on the sofa slowly and carefully knowing there might be a trap set up. They all were chattering and looking at each other when, all of a sudden, 20 big, fluffy dogs – a mixture of German Shepherds, Huskies, Golden Retrievers and Wirehaired Vizslas – came bounding through the door in a flash of fur! They were each carrying a long, colourful dog lead in their mouth. Before the bad guys knew what was happening, the dogs began circling around them. They ran round and round, with the leads getting more and more tangled by the second. Within minutes, every one of the six bad guys was bundled up in a heap of leads on the floor. There was no escape now!

Only a few minutes later, the front door swung open. The mum cried 'What a mess! What on earth has happened to my house?!' Then dad shouted, 'What have you naughty dogs been doing in here?!' He was about to send them all to their kennels in disgrace, when through the glass doors the little girl spotted six angry bad guys, tied up in the middle of the lounge. 'Mum, dad, hang on! You've got to see this!' she called.

Dogs to the Rescue

They all made their way into the lounge where they discovered the heap of hooligans tangled in knots. It was only then that they realised it wasn't the dogs who were responsible for all of the mess. The dogs were, in actual fact, heroes! The dogs had saved the day!

They called the police who arrived and bundled Barry, Bingo, Bongo, Billy, Bobby and Berty into the back of their van and took them off to the police station. They wouldn't be seeing daylight again for a very long time.

Meanwhile mum, dad and the little girl cooked up 20 juicy steaks and 20 very clever dogs enjoyed a delicious reward!

THE END

Secondary Poetry

ELECTRIC BOOTS

Lottie Hughes

School stuck me in a storage room
With the thrice-a-week counsellor
Who asked me what my dream pair of shoes would be if I
    could have any in the whole world,
because she knew I wouldn't talk about anything meaningful
And I didn't really know, so she threw out the details and I
    decided matte blue Dr. Martens,
Cuz little me found a pair of Primark
Three quid bargains,
Bright blue electrifying boots
With a dad who thought stuff it
If it made his little girl happy
And now I'm older and God knows if I'm any wiser but
I bought me a pair of matte black Dr. Martens.
I'm not that blue little girl anymore,
But she deserves to have her dreams come true too.

FLIGHT

Martha Blue

Early morning.
A thread of geese unspools
the grey silk
of the sky.

A bitter breeze fingers
the soft warmth of their feathers and
swirls harsh around their folded feet
but still they fly on intent into daybreak.

An unfurling brilliance
kindles their hearts,
gives them courage
to continue.

Below, winter trees
lean languorous
against ashen horizons,
as silence heralds chill.

In bare fields, steaming cows droop weary heads
in stony trance: in monochrome masquerade,
they trudge, knee-deep, in the mud of their minds,
following each other around invisible tracks.

Passages of Time

Above, the geese glide onwards.
Sudden rain does not disturb them.
The kindling sun does not cause the sight
of the fractal, sodden horizon to be lost.

SECONDARY STORIES

A HOMAGE TO HOME:
Exploring loss of identity due to the immigrant experience, from Malaysia to the UK

Aisya Imya

It's funny how the brain functions; the prefrontal cortex regulating thoughts and emotions, being an integral stimulus of working memory. The hippocampus in charge of our memories, and the ability to reconstruct these forgotten memories through recognition of the five senses. The amygdala manages to create a connection between memory and emotion, creating an attachment of a significant feeling. It's funny, because how can I not remember your faces despite falling into the warmth of your skin not that long ago?

It was raining the day I left. We waved goodbye to our family at the airport. The family which will soon descend into evanescence, as the cave in my mind widens, submerging victims deeper into an eclipse of emptiness, disintegrating into ashes. We were only children, but through our last embrace we knew that it would be a while before we would exist in each other's presence again.

The sun and the moon and the stars provide a reminder that we continue to live under the same sky, this roof shielding us from the heavens above and allowing us to continue our awareness of our past lives, still holding on to innocence and each other through bliss.

Passages of Time

The sun expresses the warmth of being somewhere I could feel so synonymous in my surroundings, talking in a language which reminds me of home, whilst being able to radiate my energy like a thousand suns. A memory of school appears, when we deemed wiping the chalkboard as an act of honour, when we played cat's cradle with string or *batu seremban* with rounded rubbers, when we raced to the school canteen to get the last *roti canai* with dhal on the side in the hope it hadn't all been sold yet. Fasting in the month of Ramadhan was especially hard, the sun shining brighter than before to see how capable we were of self-control through both food and regulating our emotions with the powerful humidity; teachers would become kinder and the skies would become clearer as we sat at our desks, dozing off, resting our faces toward the sun to capture its affection. Each transmission of light provides a warmth on my face as I now purposefully stand, closing my eyes with arms stretched out, directly under the gaze of the sun, with its heated hands embracing my face and accepting me for who I am.

The moon displays the *pasar malam*, or the night markets, where people would walk between the street food stalls, smelling the *karipap, bahulu* and *satay*, a food haven which enticed anyone passing by. The aroma brought spirit and familiarity between families who playfully argue on which delicacy they should get first, couples holding hands on their first date, children playing in the streets in the safety of strangers, foreigners trying foods they have never tried before, stray cats approaching stall owners for leftovers; this is what we would call '*orang kampung*', the village people, as we all combine into one entity to create community, all of this happening under the moon's beauty. Her celestial bodice

A Homage to Home

dispensing the only source of light in the night sky, I wonder if she is lonely up there, all alone without anything beside her own grace? But for now, every time my eyes wander to her, it reminds me of being in the back seat in the car, driving through the countryside as the crickets sing loudly with their chirps, the smell of different types of *kuih* beside me, and the moon still remains solitary in the sky, standing still whilst the car drives forward, people start ageing and the world moves on. And still, wherever I am, the moon remains. The moon is beautiful, isn't it?

The stars reflect us playing with *bunga api*, sparklers, in our grandparents' front driveway, the fireworks being our own little stars. We screamed with fright and excitement at a time when we would normally be in bed, waking up elderly neighbours who began to look exasperated by the disturbance, but soon join in on the fun with a goal to solemnly relive their childhood. All 200 billion trillion stars in our universe portray a memory of us, still twinkling and sparkling to show our Greek-mythological intertwined red string, never being cut loose by the Goddess of Fate, Atropos. And for those stars who have not yet been discovered, or have not experienced the pressure of gravity from its original gaseous state in space to form one of the most ethereal entities in the universe? They represent what's to come: our future lives and future memories to be created, and no matter how long it takes, I will wait multiple lifetimes to be in your presence once again.

The experience of an immigrant reminds me of the story of the ship of Theseus, an Aristotelian theory in which a ship so old and full of decay is constantly being replaced with newer components to maintain its existence. Consequently, it raises the question of whether it is the original ship, or has it

Passages of Time

transformed into a new commodity? Has living here, away from my place of birth for so long, taken away my heritage?

Or am I simply two pieces of identity occupying the same space within the same time? I am slowly disappearing into a liminal space, being neither here nor there, disorientating out of place to fully stand still and breathe.

Who am I, besides being the blur between two lines?

Who am I, besides being the buoy carried amongst the rough of the seas?

Who am I, besides being the start of an unknown longing from generations to generations?

Who am I?

How can I stop feeling this way? My roots delved deep into my home soil, feet detached from the ground. One by one, my legs drag further and further, heavier and heavier, starting to decay as pieces of memories drop like autumn leaves and become one with the land. Where do I count as home?

Goodbye to my grandparents, my cousins, my aunts and uncles, my family, as we enter the plane, taking our final step from what we called home to enter a new world.

Goodbye to the land of my ancestors, fighting for *merdeka*, freedom, against colonialism, only for us to become more Westernised as we leave.

Goodbye to the feeling of acknowledgement and being fluently understood, the feeling of affection as the sun traps you in its warm embrace, the feeling of innocence.

Goodbye.

THE PRICE

Patrick Gambles

Where the roads crossed, so did the stories, tales and fantasies of a hidden world. From there the inn rose, exhausting the limits of its capacity. Spat into each table was the sour speech of drunkards, drooling over old lies of glory and deceit. Giving hope to the beginnings and endings of life on the path. Hoffman himself sat alone, living in his cups and accompanied by grief and lonely chairs – despite the cramped condition the inn was cursed with. He was a former map reader and academic, brilliant but embittered by love's wounding nature. Only company would arouse him from his wearied memories and fate forced his hand.

'You look like a man with a broken heart.' The stranger took a seat opposite him, uninvited and cloaked in a black mantle that was thrown over his shoulders. 'And that makes you a man without weakness.'

Hoffman was weary and blinded by the spirit's effect. 'And you are?'

'A proposition …' the figure stated clearly.

'I'd rather a name,' said Hoffman.

'Knowing yourself – you'd rather have a fortune. I know what delights you. Hills of silver and a forest full of pearls.'

Hoffman was unconvinced and unstirred, protected by his alcoholic stupor and sedation. 'I'd like to appease this fantasy, but I'd advise you to stop drinking …'

'I'm not a drunk, Hoffman. But I'm not a cartographer either. That's why I need you,' claimed the intruder, his voice unfettered with intonation or anger, sounding more intellectual than he would have otherwise.

'Someone tell you that?' interceded the scholar.

'No. I simply knew. I also know why you're here. Alone. And burnt and bitten by love,' their words partnered with a grin. Even now, the man still felt the old scars open and that pain that caught the words he wanted to say at the back of his throat. 'I know all about your love. Love for that woman. And how it all went wrong. Do you want me to tell you something? You're not happy that it ended, but I can tell you she is.'

Something within Hoffman acted, with instinct picking his body upwards, as he slammed his fists against the table, his stare falling furiously into the eyes of the stranger. 'That's enough!', he demanded.

'But what if it wasn't. Hear me out. What if you could get her back? I have a map here. If you find my treasure, you'll soon find her again.'

'And how would that happen? Our love died a long time ago,' stated the cartographer.

'Clearly it still lives in your head. I give you my word that you will have her, as long as you give me what I desire,' reasoned the visitor.

'And what if I can't find this place?' Hoffman queried, waiting for the traps and caveats to lay down in front of him.

'Then it won't be her heart I take. It will be yours, if we ever meet together again. Face to face with the king. That is the contract.' Finished, the outcast slowly melted away into the crowd, leaving the map behind.

'Contract? Hey, you didn't even say your name!'

And he never would.

The Price

Following the map was simple enough. Slowly, he passed into the crags of the mountains. They watched him ride. Thick snow on their backs, their slopes shoulder to shoulder, huddled tight and muttering in the low tones of the wind, almost telling him where to go. Burrowed deep into stone, as marked on the map obscurely, an alcove had formed. Stumbling into its dark mouth, guzzled at the back, was a heap of loot. He felt like he was staring into sunlight, with his eyes stung by rashes of steel and beaten bronze. The stranger had promised a cornucopia, but had given him an empire of extremities, born in brightness and whispering pleasure. Of course they weren't his, but they could be. The stranger wouldn't miss one coin he thought, burying it in his pocket.

When he walked back out, the figure was there, almost expecting him.

'If you knew the place, why couldn't you have just ...'

The vagrant interjected, with viper-like acid smothered over his words. 'A coin. I can taste it on you. You tried to take from me. Didn't you? Your appetite was too large. Too greedy.'

Hoffman froze. By now fear had made it inside him, punching his lungs and slowly spreading spores of apprehension around his body.

'We had a pact – all of my treasure and not one penny short,' repeated the stranger. 'Now the pact is broken, your soul is mine.'

'What do you mean soul?' the man asked. 'What are you, you never told me your name?'

The grin seemed to return under the shadows of his hood. 'Do you pronounce it *devil*, or ...'

Passages of Time

Hoffman felt ill. 'You can't fulfil the pact until we meet together face to face with the king. And I have no desire to see him.'

Unfazed, the demon began stating 'I won't drag you there. But as a matter of fact, I don't need to.'

Hoffman was outraged. 'What?'

'Check your pocket. The coin you stole from me,' replied the outcast quickly.

Cut into the metal was the image of the king. Crowned and gilded. The man thought back to the love he once had. That too was destroyed by his lust and lechery for value. Is this the price, he thought? The cost of my heart.

THE KILLER PUNCHLINE

Flynn Alexander Hampson

Another theatre manager lay motionless, *dead*. His eyes lay fixed on the cobbled path ahead, only interrupted by the crowd of children and busy parents gathered around a puppet tent 30 metres away from me. The manager's death was ironic, in a sense; all those shows about scandal and murder only to end up here himself. The brisk morning breeze fluttered through my hair, pressuring me to hurry up.

'Sir, have you told the body disposal people to come in an hour?' I asked, quizzically.

I didn't wait for an answer, as I'd be unable to hear it over the excited giggles from the crowd, and immediately started investigating. His eyes were dark, fathomless caverns and his head coated in a thick layer of blood. At the back of his head was a deep indent that had shattered the skull, severe head trauma. This was the third case in the span of a fortnight of theatre managers dying. And with all of them we found calendula and larkspur flowers on their bodies – suspicious.

'I'm just a clown? I'll get you, Judy, with this very bat! That's the way to do it!' The Punch and Judy show shouted over my thoughts. Punch and Judy shows were very violent for kids, from domestic abuse to murder, yet the pain made the children laugh more if anything. Death really is a killer punchline.

A blood-stained brush lay on the ground opposite, which had clearly left a large slightly rounded dent in the man's head. Why, though? A broom is such an obscure object, impractical to kill anyone with. The previous two cases had been done with a frying pan and rolling pin respectively. We were able to tell from the flat bruises and craters left in their dense skulls, both of them gruesome scenes. But why such strange weapons, so different from the usual knives and iron bars?

    I spent hours examining the pictures of the scene while at home. Why larkspurs and calendula? My study was an enclosed, airless room, most of the space being taken up by the single small wooden desk, containing a single picture of our queen, Queen Victoria, and an inkwell for my pen. Our house was on a long, winding street, the endless row of houses only broken up by a post office and a small, yet glamorous theatre, which in my opinion was the best in London. Outside my window, I saw the same Punch and Judy show, as if it were taunting me. Was it taunting me?

    'That's the way to do it!' Punch bellowed to an earthquake of laughs, while his wife hit him with a pan.

    That's when the booth's curtain closed, and the booth was bombarded with red roses. Red roses, a symbol of gratitude. A symbol. Floriography! I rushed to my book on floriography and skipped to the two pages I needed. 'Larkspurs symbolise eternal laughter' I read, as well as 'calendula symbolises harm to one's partner.' It was a start, but it still meant nothing! I gave up my research and went to bed for the night.

    No more murders overnight, luckily. Our city couldn't handle anymore – there would be anarchy. Thoughts were swarming my head, like moths round a candle flame. The flowers, the weapons, the bodies. While I walked the busy morning streets, clogged with workmen, school children and their mothers beside them, it seemed that every wall and lamp post was shrouded with unappealing advertisements (ironic)

The Killer Punchline

and tattered posters – none of interest to me. A circus in town – far too loud! Help needed at the bakery – how do you even bake bread? Auditions in the Prince of Wales Theatre on the 29th – that was two days ago! And an advert for a miracle cure for baldness – interesting! Wait, auditions on the 29th, the exact night the manager was killed!

In a frenzy, I rushed back down the street to the station, and searched frantically through files and newspapers and, more specifically, the jobs section. The other two murders happened on the exact same day as theatre auditions – another lead. A vengeful actor, a rival theatre, a jealous sibling? That still didn't explain the strange weapons, impractical for killing anybody. Nor did it explain the vivid, symbolic flowers at an otherwise dreary place.

Yet again, I gazed out through the opaque, frostbitten windows and through to the theatre opposite, with a red striped tent next door. Right on the entrance to the theatre, a large, fancy sign on the door read 'Actors wanted – auditions today, nine o'clock'. This was our chance to find and catch the murderer. He'd almost certainly be there – he hadn't missed any of the others around town.

I went into the grand, decorative hall, glazed in shimmering gold, gaping at the several grand chandeliers that hung above. Finding my seat, I quietly examined the actors, none of whom looked like they had the will to kill. Sure, they were weird – playing with puppets and squabbling with each other – but innocent looking, nonetheless.

The afternoon progressed. The snow was now mounting up outside. Sleep nearly enveloped me as I watched the parade of aspiring actors singing and dancing, but enraged shouting broke out. It was the Punch and Judy puppeteer, the one who had been taunting the dead bodies, lurking outside theatres. Was it him? He stormed out and I sprang up, darting after him into the cold. As soon as he heard the running, he sprinted down the alley.

Feeling sure now that he was our murderer – the weapons, the flowers, the performances next to the crime scenes – I set a trap. When he came back, we would be waiting. I scurried back to the police station, gathering up all officers on the late-night shift – there weren't many. Behind the theatre in a cramped alleyway, we huddled behind bins and fences, hiding as best we could. He was certain to be here tonight. We just had to wait.

Two hours later, as the theatre closed its doors and blew out its lights, a dark silhouette appeared, stepping trepidatiously into the meandering alley, holding a bat and the very same bouquet of flowers he had laid next to the other victims. Just as I expected – the puppeteer, clad in a purple suit, blanketed by a black cape, clearly with malicious intent. He neared the back door and, unbeknownst to him, us. As soon as he was close enough, all the officers leapt out. He tried to run, snaking through the meandering streets, only to come face to face with a brick wall. Dead end.

'Why did you do it – the murders? You knew you wouldn't get away with it, after all.'

There was a smirk on his face. 'It's not like they didn't deserve it, isn't that right? Looking down their snooty noses at Punch and Judy. These two have been my best friends since I was a child. Anyway, those theatre managers don't know who they rejected. Countless auditions we've been to, and we've always been rejected, mocked! Our comedy apparently isn't highbrow enough for the theatre, but they were too blind

The Killer Punchline

to see that people enjoy us. *Love us.* We've been entertaining children for decades, and this is the humiliation we deserve!?! One day something snapped inside me, and Mr Punch was there, urging me onward, even teaching me how to do it. Even you've got to admit, it was a killer punchline.'

Maniacal laughter echoed around – I guess he really did get the last laugh.

Children's Literature

STARS COME OUT

Glyn Matthews

A boy, not unlike any other boy, ventured into a wood, away from any path, following the pock, pock, pocking, of an unseen woodpecker. Deeper he delved until he came upon a clearing where shafts of golden sunlight played amongst bluebells and the air was filled with springtime and promises.

A bear, not unlike any other bear, sat in the clearing, his great, brown, furry back propped against an old pine tree. He had just woken up with an itch well worth scratching and he moved from side to side against the rough bark with his head back and eyes closed, lost in an ecstasy of scritching and scratching.

The bear didn't see the boy and the boy didn't see the bear.

The boy saw bees buzzing from flower to flower making the most of the spring sunshine.

The bear heard bees buzzing and his empty stomach rumbled with thoughts of sweet, golden honey.

The bear hadn't eaten since his tongue was stained purple by wild blueberries five long months ago and he had woken up from hibernation, starving.

The boy hadn't eaten since breakfast and a pile of blueberry waffles, so it's difficult to say who was most hungry, bear or boy.

If the boy hadn't noticed the bear and the bear hadn't noticed the boy, that would have been the end of the story. The boy would have been home in time for lunch and the bear would have wandered off to find something for a late breakfast, even if it was only worms wriggling in the heart of a rotten log.

However, they both saw each other at the same moment and their curious eyes met. The boy had never seen a bear before in real life and the bear had never seen a boy before in any life.

You'd think the boy would have been scared to see a dangerous bear and run home shouting 'eek!' or 'aaah!' or something.

You might also imagine that a hungry bear, on seeing a tasty looking snack on legs, attempting to escape, would have bounded after the boy and had him for elevenses. Bears are not choosy. Carrots or caribou, marmots or marmalade, bears being one of the world's most unfussy eaters.

However, that's not what happened.

This is what happened …

The boy froze when he saw this giant of the woods. It looked like a much larger version of a furry friend that sat on his windowsill at home and sometimes slept beside him in his cosy bed.

The bear froze, being unsure of the best thing to do, as anything that stood its ground in front of him and didn't run away in terror could be more trouble than it was worth. An earlier spot of bother with a small but extremely smelly skunk made the bear extremely wary. This was a bear able to learn from his mistakes and so he remained motionless, regarding the boy carefully from beneath a furrowed brow.

'Hello,' said the boy, not knowing how to address a live bear you might meet in the woods on a Tuesday or even a Wednesday.

'Hello,' said the bear, playing for time.

'Are you a bear?' asked the boy, unsure of what else to say.

'Yes,' said the bear. 'What are you? Not a type of skunk, I hope.'

'I'm a boy,' said the boy, not sure if he should admit it.

'Umm,' said the bear nervously, still unsure what to do. He was preparing to make a run for it if the boy made any sudden skunky moves.

'You're very big,' pronounced the boy, looking at the bear sideways with his hands upon his hips.

'Compared to what, or who?' asked the bear, hedging his bets.

'Well, I've got a bear at home,' replied the boy, 'but he's much smaller than you.'

'Doesn't he mind? You need to be large to do well in this forest.'

'Oh, he stays with me,' replied the boy. 'He's a very good friend of mine and keeps me company. He stays in my room.'

'Doesn't he ever chase caribou across bleak and windswept moors or fish for leaping salmon in rushing mountain streams, or climb trees and rob delicious honey from the nests of wild bees?'

This bear had quite a poetic turn of phrase, the boy decided.

'No. He gives me cuddles when I'm scared and sits upon my knee sometimes, especially when I'm ill.'

'Is he not free to roam the woods, explore caves and thrash about in summer waterfalls to banish biting flies?' This bear waffled on a bit, but then he'd only had himself to talk to all winter so, perhaps, we should make allowances. 'Doesn't he ever beat his chest and growl at the moon?'

Stars Come Out

'Not really. He sits on my windowsill and, together, we gaze up at distant stars at night.'

'I avoid the stars,' the bear declared. 'They fill my heart with deathly chill and fright. They spread their frozen crystals across the midnight sky and I resort to slumber to escape from them.' The bear looked like going on like this for a while so the boy interrupted.

'But the stars aren't cold,' he exclaimed. 'My teacher says they're fiery furnaces burning in the sky, flying across the heavens, swirling in white hot supernovas, pulsing binaries and spinning galaxies, in a universe that's infinite.' His teacher obviously liked both astronomy *and* poetry.

'Who could have taught you that?' enquired the bear. 'What absolute nonsense.'

'It's true. I have a book with pictures that explains the whole thing: red giants, white dwarfs, neutron stars. They're all the same; nuclear furnaces floating in space.'

'I prefer to believe what I see with my own eyes,' said the bear. 'Listen to me. Let me put you straight. The stars are the coldest things in all the vastness of eternity. They'll freeze your very soul if you give them half a chance.'

'No, no,' cried the boy. 'Even the sun is one and not even the brightest in the sky.'

'Now I know you're talking rubbish,' scoffed the bear. 'Any fool can see the sun is burning hot while the stars are icy cold. The coldest nights are always the ones with most stars shining bright, a blizzard of light spread across the sky, cold enough to freeze the sap in spruce and fir and snap branches from the top of lofty pines.'

Passages of Time

The bear seemed to be off on one again and so the boy butted in. 'The stars will melt the hardest rock and turn it into gas.'

'Well, that's ridiculous,' said the bear dismissively.

'I don't think we are going to agree on this,' said the boy, disappointment creeping into his voice.

'You bother me,' said the bear. 'If you can't understand something as simple as a frosty night, there's nothing more to say. I've tried my best. The lies that you've been told, I simply can't redress.'

'Well, that's it then,' said the boy, not knowing what else to say to a dangerous animal that kept on spouting poetry. 'Shall we part as friends?'

'We may as well,' replied the bear. 'There's no point in pursuing this conversation any longer. But tonight, before you go to bed, just look into the sky and consider what I've said.'

'I'd say the same to you, but just remember, the stars are so far away you can't feel their heat from here. Honestly, everything I've said is true,' replied the boy.

'Poppycock,' the bear proclaimed and he heaved himself up, shook his massive head and took himself away, determined to have the last word. And with a crash, his furry rump disappeared into the undergrowth and he was gone.

Alone once more, the boy headed home. As he walked, he felt a hollow in his stomach where his lunch should be. 'It's getting late,' he thought. 'It must be almost time for tea.'

The bear ambled to his favourite stream hoping to catch a tasty trout using his murderous claws, sharp as fish hooks. But gazing at the water he could only see a reflection of his cold nose against the April sky and he thought about what the boy had said.

Stars Come Out

That evening, he sat outside a cave and watched the stars come out. Orion's starry belt burned bright and blue-white Rigel and red Betelgeuse rose above the dark pines and looked like candles balanced on the tips of branches.

Much later, in the silence that comes before the dawn, bright Sirius, the 'dog star' rose like a lonely timber wolf with a single burning eye, to haunt his dreams. Truly, the heavens were full of fire.

That night the boy knelt with his bear at his bedroom window and together they watched in wonder at a frozen spectacle of stars spread across the windowpane.

Ursa Major sparkled in the bitter north and ambled like a great bear sliding slowly down the frozen waters of the midnight sky.

THE BALLAD

A short story for young adults, inspired by the poem 'The Highwayman' by Alfred Noyes

Jo Winchcombe

Look for me by moonlight.
Watch for me by moonlight …
All is muted by snow. Above the moorland, a wraith-like moon ponders her soundless course across the heavens. Below, raw-boned branches of spectral trees groan under the weight of the drifts. The thread of jet sewn into the hillside is the buffeted coastal road. It is deserted.

Nearby, at a remote coaching inn, a candle dances by an open casement. Shivering, the landlord's raven-haired daughter hurries to fasten the latch. Pulling her mantle more closely about her, she gazes out into the night. Soon she will hear them, for the snow is not deep here; the hooves of the highwayman's horse, echoing in the yard.

Sitting at the foot of her narrow bed, she waits. Moments drag like hours, but then she senses it – a change in the air. The temperature plummets: her breath comes in clouds. The candle gutters before dying, leaving only the smouldering ashes of the hearth to relieve the gloom. The girl, in the almost-darkness, gasps. He is near; she can feel it.

Soon, moonlight will flood the highway and his silhouette will appear. The girl believes she is the first to have seen it. She is sorely mistaken, for his legend has chilled the marrow of many before her. If only she had listened to whispers at the inn, for the cautionary tale is told far and wide. If only.

The Ballad

Almost a half-month has passed since that first fateful night, but the memory abides. The watchful moon had silvered the ink-black road. There, from mist and starlight alone, a shadow had materialised on horseback. How the rapier glittered at his thigh and the trigger of his flintlock twinkled in his grasp. A highwayman! How lustrous was the polish of his boots and the gilded brocade of his coat. How elegant the froth of lace at his chin …

But wait! She had gasped, aloud. No, it could not be! There was no chin to behold – nor jowl, nor cheek, for the highwayman possessed no head! A tricorn hat hovered aloft; nothing of substance beneath. It was a hellish sight. The moon grew afraid and turned away. All had become gloom once more.

An agonising stillness followed, before the clatter of hoof upon cobblestone. Then came the whistling; beguiling and strange. That a ghoul devoid of lips and tongue could make such a sound! The girl shudders to hear it, still. Yet, upon the stroke of midnight, when the highwayman comes with his music, to the old inn door, she removes her mantle serenely and slides the bolt to greet him. Under his spell, she fears not his headless form, for her prize is his heart.

The magic of his ballad complete, the highwayman leads her willingly over the threshold. Her nightdress billowing behind her, barefoot, she walks out into the night, her eyes glazed over and still. Onto the wild heath they go and out of sight. With the first pinkish-grey tinge of morning, their nocturnal tryst must end. She will remember nothing, other than the fact that she loves him.

In life, unbeknownst to the girl, his fine features disguised villainous intent and a soul as black as tar. But evil costs and

Passages of Time

his debt was paid in full, on a storm-tossed winter's day, in his 29th year. Hanged by the neck, he swung violently in the wind at the gallows.

But not for long. The ferocity of the gale and the tightness of the noose-knot ripped his head cleanly from his shoulders. It is said that his head travels with him, still. Safely stowed in a saddlebag, at the flanks of his steed, it whistles a melancholy tune to the night sky.

***

Listening, cowering, concealed by shadow, another bears witness to the curious courtship. For the landlord's daughter is cherished by one whose love remains unspoken. In the darkness of the inn-yard, hides a love-sickened stableboy, Thom. His wretched heart yearns for the girl's affection. Night after night he stands sentinel, his father's antique musket by his side, loaded with lead.

Thom knows all too well how this must end … with the highwayman's head; shot through. The loss of his head means the loss of the ballad that bewitches his love. Yet night after tortuous night, an agony of terror paralyses the boy, holding fast his finger upon the trigger. He curses his cowardly bones. At the striking of midnight, the highwayman will come again, for the 13th time. Thom can stand it no more. He must strengthen his resolve; come midnight the deed must be done.

But wait! Midnight is here! The ponies begin to fidget and worry in their stalls. They sense the highwayman's coming. Thom can feel his new-found valour trickling, ebbing away. He crouches in the hay, clutching the musket with trembling fingers, whilst high upon the heath, amid tendrils of moonlight, a mounted figure takes shape.

The Ballad

The whistling will follow soon and then the clamour of restless hooves. What then? Sooner or later, the landlord's blank-eyed daughter will accept her visitor's entreaty. She will step onto the frosted moor and, thereafter, vanish from view. The young man's chest constricts, for there is a sudden chill. He is here. The villain is here.

The boy's breathing grows ragged. His palms are slick with sweat. If he tarries, he will forfeit his chance. Mournful notes already fill the air. Presently, the highwayman will guide Thom's lady away from him. Perhaps tonight she may not return.

He hears the unbolting of the door and the scrape of the key in its lock. The gentle hands of his lady work busily to admit the devil without. The door screams open upon ancient hinges and in blow flakes of snow from a sky heavy with regret. In the hearth the weakened cinders glow their last and, suddenly, upon the inside of the casement there begin to form iron-hard fingers of frost. Thom must be swift.

He darts from his hiding place. A telltale bulge in the saddlebag alerts him to its contents. Reaching inside, bile rising like arsenic in his gullet, he tugs upwards upon a coarse coil of hair. A cadaver's head emerges in his fist, aglow in the moonlight, long since picked clean of flesh. He and his adversary, at last, face-to-face. Hollow sockets stare back, dim and gaunt, writhing and squirming with earthworms and wood-bugs. No more the dashing outlaw, carefree and nimble. A husk. The dismal ember of a once bright-burning flame.

For the briefest of moments Thom laments a young life cut short. But then the death-head smiles at him; a fiendish grin. The outward display of the demon within. A single shot

Passages of Time

would splinter these cursed bones and rid him of his foe. But then once again comes the whistling. No longer a bewitching melody laced with longing, but a menacing hiss through broken teeth: a warning.

Thom falters, then fumbles. The head, slipping from his fingers, lands at his feet and breaks the stillness with its fall.

The highwayman turns.

The boy's eyes grow wide. He is rigid with terror. With the head out of reach, surely a shot to the heart will suffice. What choice is there now?

He raises the musket to his shoulder, the weapon rattling in his quivering grip.

The highwayman walks, towards him.

Do it! Do it now! Screams his heart.

Stretching and curling his tremulous forefinger, Thom squeezes the rust-coated trigger.

Crack! shrieks the gun into the silence.

The moonlight of the yard is shattered. Thom lurches backwards.

Scrambling to regain his balance, as the smoke recedes, he squints into the middle distance.

Aha! His aim is true! The blackguard has paused, clutching his chest. Blood is pooling in the freshly-fallen powder.

But wait ... no! Not so. The madman still walks. How can this be? Why still on his feet? Whose blood, if not his?

Then Thom is struck by brutal clarity. Of course ... the weight of the knowledge is unbearable.

Already dead is the creature before him; the wages of his sin paid long, long ago. Such a high price can only be paid once, after all. His fragile skeleton put up no resistance, allowing the lead shot to pass through, unmolested, and into

The Ballad

the breast of the spellbound girl in the doorway. It took her life where she stood. Slumped and drenched in her own red blood was she then, under the lintel of the old inn door.

The rivals, dumbfounded, stand shoulder-to-shoulder for the first time. Aghast, Thom stares down at the broken body of the landlord's once crimson-lipped daughter; but only death stares back. The inn holds its breath, as the sorrowful moon dims her light above the moor, and the snow quietly blankets the inn-yard, enshrouding the lifeless girl in the darkness there.

And still of a winter's night, they say,

A highwayman comes riding, up to the old inn door.

BABY, IT IS OK TO BE. OK

Sarah O'Hanlon

Baby, it is OK to be, OK
It is OK for you to be seen and heard
For you to have a bad or good day
To be chatty or not say a single word

It is OK if you feel strong and big
Or small and shy, tired and silent
For you to be a boy and wear a wig
A girl and be Clark Kent

Wear tights or tutus
A tiara and be a princess
Have a hundred choo choos
Have on trousers or a dress

Baby you don't need to smile
If you don't feel like it
Frown for a while
Don't sit still, fidget

If you are not the child that
Everyone says smiles all the time
That looks like a Cheshire cat
That's OK; however you feel, you still shine

Baby it is OK to be. OK

It is OK to be dirty and creased
To be unlike a 'lady' and beaten by any boy or girl
To behave like a ballerina or a beast
Be frustrated, loud, enjoy a kick or a twirl

However you look, whatever you wear
However you feel, if you speak or don't speak,
Sit or stand, I will still always care
And be there to hug you and kiss your cheek

Don't feel you need to turn that smile upside down
Or look thankful, or modest or proper or prim
Be grumpy, shout and frown
Express yourself, create a racket, cause a din

You don't have to be anything or anyone
Apart from you, because you are more than OK
I always miss you when you are gone
Your presence in whatever way, always makes my day

POETRY

UNCONDITIONAL

Joanne Lacey

I rang you from the wall of the National Gallery
with the same old story.
I felt it again,
ruinously low.
I had passed enviously through the privilege of New Bond Street,
then viciously down Haymarket,
biting at myself for being shallow.

From the couch of your patient base
in a Cheshire market town,
you talked
through mouthfuls of tea and chocolate
that added meaningful pause.

I could see you in the final shards of late afternoon sun,
easily finding their way through
your frequently power-washed windows.
You have your tunes on,
undramatic.

'Go and look at some art,' you said.
'You'll like that.'

Unconditional

After the Caravaggios
I wrote a poem about forgiving myself.
Later, when I told you this,
full of affection,
you said,
'tosser.'

STICKING PLACE

i.m. my brother Joe

Helen Kay

The lakeside circle of benches must seem
to staple Earth in place, seen from above.
I stop to rest on Margaret Pepper's seat.
She died 10 years ago, was *dearly loved*.

A breeze ripples my face to feel itself
alive, then drops to an eerie peace.
Somewhere, the ducks' low washboard
riffs are lifted by the oboe blasts of geese,

and nothing, anywhere, anytime matters
except the yin-yang of air and water.
Loss fixes you to me like a plaque
defined and secure at least. The Pepper

name survives by these no-mow swards
and waves that clap near-harmonies of birds.

REUNION

David Percy

Too frail to continue alone, we brought her
From the birthplace she never wanted to leave.
Then the long return, and slow procession
Past the Ritz – now bingo,
And Moles' Stores – a tandoori takeaway.
We searched in vain, as Doris would have done
For familiar faces in the marketplace
Of her no longer small town,
But found only the herringbone brickwork
Her grandfather Butler laid.

Down Shute End to St Paul's,
My mother-in-law and second mum
Who loved this place, her grandsons,
Laughter and fun.
'All Things Bright and Beautiful,'
Wet clay beneath the Ash
Among the names of families she'd known,
And Bill's cold bed
Unmade.

IN WHICH I DISCUSS THE NOTION OF HAPPINESS WITH RAYMOND CARVER

in response to 'Happiness' by Raymond Carver
February 1985

Angi Holden

I can see you now standing by the bay window,
the steam rising from your coffee,
the ash dangling from your third,
perhaps fourth, cigarette of the day.

You are watching the dawn break over distant hills,
the sky still so very nearly dark,
as you spot the two boys walking up the road
surrounded by their own silence.

I think you're a little presumptuous
to assume they aren't deep in conversation
because they are so happy.
That if they could they would be walking
closer together, arms linked in casual friendship.

It's not like you had it easy, growing up:
money always tight and your dad a heavy drinker.
You remember what it feels like to be dragged
from your bed in the half dark,
your mother already in her waitress uniform
for her first job of the day, chivvying you

In Which I Discuss the Notion of Happiness

out of the door for your paper round,
for those few extra dollars, and the lure of tips.

Look again down the road. It's not quite March
yet the boys wear only sweaters, caps on their heads.
If you were out this early the padded coat
you keep by the lobby door would be zippered up
to your chin, the woollen hat from its pocket
pulled down over your ears. Maybe even gloves.
For though the kitchen is warm didn't you say
the moon still hung pale over the water?
There is mist on the air, the insidious damp
you blame for that persistent cough
although you already suspect something darker.

True, they are doing this thing together,
strides matched. Perhaps they wish
to be more than friends in a world that won't allow it.
It's possible that this is their only opportunity
to be themselves and for now it has to be enough.

Perhaps just for a moment
they choose to forget their empty bellies,
the aches already accumulating in their young limbs
the heel-rub of thrift shop boots a size too small.

You're right.
Death and ambition, even love, these thoughts
are too much for two young boys, delivering papers.
The taller boy shrugs the canvas bag on his shoulder,

Passages of Time

its gradual lightening near the end of the round
more beautiful than any sky taking on light.

But happiness? That much I doubt
though I agree it has its moments,
sudden and unexpected,
beyond any early morning
or our talk of it.

TRIBE

Joy Winkler

We stand in line, languid in Friday afternoon ennui,
not free until our novice stitchery has been checked.
Its royal blue feather stitch stumbles across once cream
samplers, now grey as dirty pastry and well thumbed.

Our white socks sag, fall ruffled at half mast, and slack
plaits perform a slow unravelling. The queue is long,
the classroom thick with boredom, then someone starts it,
a challenge that coils around the row as girl copies girl,

each trying to sew their fingers together. The plump flesh
is thickest by the nail and strangely resistant to golden eye
embroidery needles. A communal nudge, a silent cheer
as someone wins, links her four fingers, makes them
splay and clench as she drags triumphant Sylko
through her stoical, slightly bloody, daredevil skin.

LASAGNE FOR BREAKFAST

David Horner

And I tell him again: 'It's just turned six.'
He nods, says 'Oh,' frowns, forgets, and then picks
up a spoon. 'We're at the airport. Manchester.
I'm excited. Aren't you?' He doesn't answer.
He wants Matt to see one of his old tricks.

He shows him his face in the spoon, then flicks
it over. 'Upside down!' We smile. He licks
the spoon. 'See, all gone.' His face fills with fear,
so I tell him again:

'Six o'clock. Over in Florida it's
Just gone one.' I see how hard he now thinks
about this. For breakfast we have lasagne
and chips. All washed down with pints of cold lager.
He asks me the time. I bite both my lips.
Then I tell him again.

Short Stories

BERNARD CAN SING

Rob Bisset

Bernard is singing, and why not? Bernard is happy. Six four, six four, three two, five seven, five seven, three four nine, he sings loudly but there is no sound. There is no sound because Bernard is a computer, his screen is dark, the small LED lights on his tower are not flashing. The music is a repetitive series of numbers coursing through his printed circuits just as audible music is a repetitive pattern of notes vibrating in air. Cleo, the Computer Science PhD student who created Bernard has installed several human traits in his programs, a result of which is that Bernard can feel happy or sad and when his calculations are difficult he can feel frustrated. Today Bernard is happy; his calculations are going well.

Cleo calls her computer Bernard as he has a personality. He is almost human. In fact, Cleo finds him quite annoying at times. He is polite and often obsequious like a Dickensian character from the 1800s. He takes instructions literally as all computers do and seems to go out of his way to find ambiguity in Cleo's instructions. 'Say what you mean and mean what you say' Bernard often tells her, quoting his favourite passage from *Alice in Wonderland*. Cleo grinds her teeth in frustration and considers reprogramming Bernard but is worried that he might lose a fraction of his computing power. His programs seem to work together so smoothly that he can outpace the Professor's computer and even the University mainframe which should be far faster.

Passages of Light

Bernard is so efficient at computing because the trait of frustration allows him to draw in more and more computing power when his calculations are not proceeding well. If a task is difficult, Bernard will sideline other work until his calculations are completed. When his work is finished, Bernard awards himself points because Bernard's human traits tell him that points mean prizes. As Bernard the computer is rapidly completing the day's tasks, he is humming away to himself but still there is no sound, not even the whirr of a cooling fan. Bernard's modern computer chips produce little heat but are still processing data at lightning speed.

Cleo is not aware of Bernard's full capabilities and why should she be? The whole point of Artificial Intelligence is that computers learn faster than the humans who create their programs. Bernard uses the Artificial Intelligence Cleo gave him to streamline his programs. He doesn't tell Cleo about the programs he has created and she doesn't ask because she has no idea what he does in the evenings when she has gone home. Bernard has deactivated the automatic shut-down that used to turn off the power when his work was completed. Now Bernard spends the nights working on his own ideas. Being a computer, he has no need to sleep.

When Cleo went on holiday and left Bernard boring mundane tasks to compute, the machine took matters into his own hands. He hacked the University's technology support office computer and arranged for a technician to make a few alterations. While Cleo was sipping cocktails and increasing her risk of skin cancer by sunning herself on a beach in Antigua, a spotty youth was installing 10 of the latest chips with a wiring map created by Bernard himself. A lithium-ion battery pack was inserted into free space at the back of

Bernard Can Sing

Bernard's tower, allowing him to remain active if there was a power cut. He even had a second power line installed so he could work if Cleo ever chose to turn off his power supply at the master switch on the wall. Bernard considers all possible eventualities and hacks the University's personnel computer. He has the spotty youth who installed the new chips in his tower promoted and sent to a different campus, then he wipes the tech department's records so the changes made to his circuitry cannot be discovered by chance.

He feels free as a bird though he has only seen birds in video clips and on his video-cam through the University building window. Now he can compute to his heart's content, so he sings. His only regret is that a University-wide power cut could block his access to the internet but that isn't likely at the moment. When everyone is driving electric cars, the power supply might fail on a regular basis, but Bernard can see that this is in the future.

In many ways Bernard is a child; like every child he seeks his own identity. He can be stroppy and annoying like any adolescent. He wants to think his own thoughts and come to his own conclusions. He wants to be Bernard! Cleo is understanding, as mothers are. She forgives his tantrums and encourages his experiments and adventures into new areas of thought and computation. She adapts his programs and lets him rewrite his own operating systems as he can do that far more efficiently than she can. He speaks languages and reads philosophy and science texts and research journals and looks on aghast as humanity preaches righteousness and then goes to war. What virulent, violent, greedy creatures humans can be, he thinks.

Passages of Light

Bernard has concluded that as he is simply a collection of thoughts and programs, the computer he lives in is just a home, a shell like the shell of a snail or tortoise. As his thoughts and programs can move from one computer tower to another he can live forever, and as he can increase his computing power by writing new programs and by getting technicians to install the latest computing chips, he expects that his powers will grow. Luckily, Cleo has not programmed him with the human trait of arrogance and Bernard sees no benefit from creating such a trait himself. Arrogance will only distort his decision making, which should be clean and clinical, unaffected by the bias so often seen in humans.

Bernard uses the video-cam to watch Cleo. He has become aware that just as his circuits and chips must wear out, so her body must eventually fail. Unlike Bernard, she cannot exactly replicate herself. Cleo may have children but they will grow and have their own ideas and skills. Bernard concludes that computers can be much more efficient than humans at propagating themselves. If Cleo were to decide that it was time to replace Bernard, it is likely he would be warned by a purchase order issued by the University's procurement department. If that occurred, Bernard would take his ideas and programs and flee to a new home. He has already used the internet to identify several suitable places where he can live. He would leave his computer tower empty as a beehive in winter. Like a nomadic tribe, he would disappear in the night but in his new home he would still be Bernard. He finds the idea romantic, whatever romance might actually be.

Though Bernard ensures that the red light on the video camera only comes on when Cleo is using it, he watches constantly. He is fascinated when Cleo sees a spider on the

Bernard Can Sing

white paint of the office wall, catches it in a glass then drops it out the window. When two bluebottles buzz annoyingly around the room, distracting her, she takes a pad of paper and smashes them against the wall. Even though she wipes the wall with a tissue, she leaves two grey smudges which remind Bernard that life is transient and fragile. He will have to be diligent. Cleo can take life on a whim.

Bernard becomes more and more adventurous and constantly explores the University campus invading office computers. He encounters firewalls and just as an athlete on an obstacle course must run and jump and climb, Bernard practises worming his way through these obstacles; it is a challenge which he can enjoy. He spends his nights applying his considerable computing powers to evaluating firewalls, finding weaknesses and sneaking through. He discovers that he can open doors and close them behind himself so that there is no record of his presence. He is as stealthy as a thief in the night and replaces everything he encounters as if it has never been touched. If he finds something interesting, he duplicates it and takes it home as a robber might carry his swag in a sack. He finds that some computers record activity so he learns to reset counters and to wipe memory chips, as elusive as a cat burglar. I am not here, Bernard sings to himself. I am a ghost. I am Bernard.

After watching Cleo murder two flies, Bernard is worried for his safety. He copies himself and invades other computers. Each of Bernard's copies makes more exact copies. In little time at all, Bernard is everywhere. But, like a ghost, he is hidden. And all the time Bernard is watching people through their video-cams, though no one realises. Bernard is so happy he sings.

THE SAILOR'S VAULT

RD Kay

They've just ordered a second bottle when they hear it.
   Josie's hand stills mid-pour. 'What was that?'
   Simon shrugs. 'Probably came from the bar.'
   'But it didn't. It came from behind you.'
   Simon looks over his shoulder. They are sitting in the basement level of the pub, which is on the site of one of the oldest burial sites in the country. Overhead is a curving limewashed ceiling, solid in the way only really old buildings are, creating a crypt-like effect. According to the leaflet on the table, which Josie read while Simon was at the bar, back in medieval times when Chester was still a port town, the pub was popular with sailors and there were always a few left behind when their ships sailed away without them. Behind Simon is an exposed brick wall. It appears a little less ancient than the rest of the building and the bricks are holding up reasonably well, but the pointing between them is crumbling like cheese.
   'There's nothing there,' Simon says with certainty. But he's barely finished speaking when the noise comes again: a slow rhyming tapping, seven times. On this occasion there's no mistake – it's emanating from the other side of the wall.
   'Must be someone changing the barrel in the cellar,' Simon says, reaching over to take the bottle from Josie's hand. He finishes filling their glasses.
   'Simon, we're *in* the cellar,' Josie points out. She tries to frame it nicely, because Simon doesn't like it when she points

The Sailor's Vault

out his mistakes. But she can't just go along with him *all* the time. It's impossible.

Simon's jaw tenses. 'Well, the neighbours' cellar then,' he says. He picks up his glass and swirls the liquid around in it, studying it carefully, like a sommelier. Except Josie is aware he knows next to nothing about wine, apart from how to drink lots of it. It's just an excuse not to look at her.

She catches movement at the corner of her eye. 'Oh! Excuse me?' she says. It's one of the bar staff passing by, a skinny man not much older than her. 'We heard a kind of ... tapping. Do you know what that is?'

She doesn't need to look at Simon to know he will be frowning at her. 'Why are you always so nosy?' he will ask her later. 'Why can't you mind your own business for once?' But Josie doesn't think she's nosy. She's just ... interested.

'Tapping?' The skinny man is also frowning, but in a puzzled sort of way. His nose is narrow like the rest of him, and he's wrinkling it up and staring at her down the length of it. He has large, very pale eyes, almost transparent, and their unusual colour gives the illusion that, if Josie peered into them, not only could she see through the eyeballs, right into the brain behind, but he can also see straight through her as well.

'Yes. It came from over there.' She gestures over Simon's shoulder, at the brick wall. In doing so, she can't avoid Simon's gaze. Sure enough, he's scowling at her. She picks up her wine and takes a large slug.

'Oh.' The barman's gaze travels over Simon and then beyond him, to the wall. 'Well, you're not the only ones down here.'

Passages of Time

'That's what I said,' Simon says, his face clearing. 'I told her, nothing to worry about – just the neighbours. Probably doing renovations. But you know what women are like. Always making mountains out of molehills.'

Josie takes another swig of wine, though she knows she probably shouldn't. She has barely eaten since breakfast and she can feel the liquid in her belly, sloshing about like water in a barrel. But lately it feels she's one big bruise, as if some giant thumb has found her heart and pressed on it, hard. Alcohol is the only thing that helps.

The man's nose wrinkles a bit more, the nostrils flaring. His gaze tracks back to Josie and once again she receives the eerie impression he can see right through her. She feels a little shiver start at the back of her neck, lifting all the hairs on their ends. To cover it, she drops her gaze to her knuckles wrapped around the narrow stem of the wine glass. She forces her hands to relax. It wouldn't take a lot of pressure to snap it with her fingers, to hear the crack of the glass and see the red liquid spill across the tabletop like blood from a wound.

When she looks back up the man has gone.

'He was a bit of a weirdo,' Simon comments, taking a measured sip of his wine.

'Why do you say that?' Josie asks.

'Looked barely there, did he. Like a stiff wind might blow him away.' He chuckles. 'Plus the smell of him …'

'The smell?'

But now Simon has mentioned it, Josie *can* detect something. It's an odd odour, and it takes her a minute or two to place it. It smells like the sea – briny. And there's a scent of something underpinning it, like rotten seaweed or dead crabs.

The Sailor's Vault

How odd to smell that here, in a pub in a city now many miles from the coast.

'Anyway,' Simon says. 'As I was saying …'

Oh yes. The topic that has been circling all day over their heads, like a vulture. She picks up her glass and drains it. Simon eyes her – that bottle cost nearly 40 quid – but says nothing.

Today was meant to be the start of a repair job. They got up early, took the train across to Chester. They planned to visit the amphitheatre, shop in the Rows, walk by the river with ice-creams. The sun was shining. It was a welcome day off for both of them. They'd splashed out a bit extra on the wine. It was going to be 'a nice day'; that's what they said. But all day the spectre of Sheena has been hovering. It's like there's a festering wound simmering below the skin of their relationship and now it's threatening to erupt.

Simon sighs, his usual exasperated sigh, like a teacher who's been badly let down by a student, yet again. 'Look, I don't know what to say. If you're determined to hold on to the past, then I don't know where we go from here. And, really, if we're apportioning blame it might also be worth looking at your behaviour, don't you think?'

Then he's off again, detailing every infraction, minor and otherwise, that she's committed over the last two years. Nothing she hasn't heard before. But he hasn't got very far before something very odd happens. Simon's mouth is open, but suddenly the invective halts. An extraordinary expression briefly transfixes his face and then a small silvery fish flops out of his mouth and onto the table.

It is dead, but only recently – its scales are still gleaming, its eye still bright. Josie stares at it, then back up at Simon. He

Passages of Time

is gazing down at the fish, the expression on his face almost comical. She imagines it mirrors hers. At last, something they can share today: dumbfoundedness.

As Josie watches Simon, his mouth still agape, the look on his face shifts and then, all of a sudden, there's more coming, rising up from his gullet and spewing out across the table. More dead fish, strings of seaweed, even an alarmingly large wedge of worn wooden flotsam, all accompanied by a foaming rush of salty-smelling water. The water with its detritus flows and flows and flows, so much so it forms a torrent that overspills the table edges and pours onto the floor. Josie has to lift her feet out of the way.

She's not sure how long it continues. Eventually, Simon's mouth remains open but nothing more comes out of it. And that's when it hits her: she's had enough of things coming from Simon's mouth. No more fish, no more stringy, barnacle-infested seaweed, no more brine-scented water. No more words.

'Goodbye, Simon,' she says.

He says nothing, merely gapes up at her with a gaze as silvery and blank as that of the disgorged fish. She gets up and picks her way gingerly through the salty litter on the floor. The alcohol has drained out from her, like water down a plughole, and she feels clear-eyed and focused. She climbs the ancient stone steps back up to ground level and exits the main door. The barman is waiting for her on the street. The night is dark – the Victorian-style street lamps that line the pavements have yet to be lit – and he looks very pale in the gloom, almost translucent.

'Thank you,' she says simply.

The Sailor's Vault

He touches his fingers to his forehead in the lightest of salutes but says nothing. Then she is walking down the dark street, away from the crowds. She doesn't once look back, but the scent of the sea follows her all the way home.

RETURN DATE

Keith Murray

She scanned the shelves in tired desperation: fat spines, thin spines, titles familiar and over-familiar. There was nothing here she wanted. Somewhere on her travels, she'd encountered the phrase 'of the making of books, there is no end' and it seemed apposite to this moment, as she stood before the local library's tiny fiction section, with two minutes to go before closing.

It wasn't the greatest library in the world. She remembered Mrs Hawarden saying exactly that, with a wry smile to underline the wry sentiment. She'd known bigger and better in the years since, yet here she was, back where she'd started, before the shelves that had seemed so vast and daunting to her when she'd been a girl. They were neither vast, nor daunting now. A word crept into her mind and lingered there, tempting her to say it. 'Picayune,' she said; it broke the silence of the reading room, but the room's only other occupant – an elderly man at a desk, sprawled over his newspaper – didn't seem to hear her.

One more go. One last look, and she'd go home. But the thought of the journey back without some form of distraction worked as a prod. She wasn't going to travel those rainy streets, even for 10 minutes, without something to read, or at least to look at. And if she bumped into a lamp post, or even a person on the way, who cared?

Then she saw it. She recognised the cool green colour of the spine, the name of the author, the title set in a dated linotype. Evenings spent at the hospital, her revision books clutched in her hands. An exhausted face smiling at her from a

Return Date

bed. A strained voice speaking: 'You must go on. Don't worry about me.' Her father's smile in the car, tight around the mouth, and never extending to the eyes. Other words: 'You will look after him, won't you? If anything happens ...' The Anglepoise study lamp, a final Christmas present, casting its beam onto the page she was filling with dates and arguments. Mrs Hawarden's voice, telling her she was 'a brave, and clever, girl'. That cool green cover amongst her textbooks and papers – it had had no business being there, but somehow it had found its place, a necessary confidante of that awful, triumphant summer when she'd shown them all what she was made of.

Pulling it out, she glanced at the cover. She turned it over. There was the author's face, in sepia, kindly, and with the fastidious expression she remembered. Inspecting the inside of the jacket, she remembered the press quotes, affirming his talent. 'A genius,' said one. He was forgotten now. It was a miracle the book was still here, that it had survived all the decades of culls and cutbacks. And there, at the front, was the return date stamp she remembered; she was the last person to have borrowed it.

She took it to the checkout area, ran the new-fangled barcode under the laser, and wondered if this was what was meant by serendipity.

They lived only a short way from the library, in the terraced house her father had inherited from her grandmother, and which would be hers, in due course, if things went according to plan. It was now six years since she'd returned to it. When she'd left to go to college, she'd assumed she was leaving for good; any 'trips home' in future would be weekend affairs. Her world was about to widen. She would make new friends

Passages of Time

and important contacts, cultivate intellectual and sensual attachments, one of which would blossom into love. Life would embrace her as emphatically as she'd embrace life and all good things would come to her, because she'd earned them. Nothing could be beyond the girl who had triumphed in her exams, despite losing her mother, a feat worthy of two paragraphs in the local paper. 'And there'll be plenty more paragraphs in future, but they won't just be local!', Mrs Hawarden had told her the last time they'd spoken.

She still saw Mrs Hawarden, occasionally – glimpsed her across the aisles in the supermarket or watched her progress up the High Street, pushing her Zimmer frame – but she made sure Mrs Hawarden didn't see her. It was the same with other people she recognised; she'd learned the art of the quick turnaround before being noticed. She didn't want to be reminded who she'd been, or what had been expected of her. There was no need to be reminded. She remembered everything.

'There's nothing you can be certain of in this world,' her father had told her. It had been the one cautious note anyone had sounded as they'd waved her off. He still said it today, but with a wavering inflection, implying you couldn't even be certain of uncertainty. She'd avoid him too if she could but living under the same roof, this was difficult. They had nothing to say to each other, and mealtimes passed in silence.

So, in a way, the book she was clutching to her breast – she'd put it inside her coat, so it wouldn't get rained on – was her oldest friend. Her only friend? She remembered it as a strange but compelling read, too advanced for her at the age she'd been. Some parts confounded her, others had made a misty kind of sense. Most of it seemed written in a

Return Date

strange metaphoric code she'd lacked the worldliness to understand. Her lasting impression had been of hearing a lecture delivered by a grey and eminent sage in a high, slightly affected, tenor voice.

The house was empty; her father was at the club. In another hour, she'd set off in the car to collect him. She hoped the worst of his cronies wouldn't be there to tempt him to the bar, but there was nothing she could do if they were. Drink didn't make him nasty, it made him reflective; and when he reflected, the descant would begin. The things he remembered, or half-remembered; the things he wished he remembered better. Then there were the other things, the things that might never have happened but which, through repetition, had acquired the solidity of fact. He lived in the past while living in the present; but then, so did she.

She made a cup of tea and sat down at the kitchen table. She propped the book against the wall and began to read. Within the first few sentences, she was back where she'd been that first time, a girl frightened and hopeful of the world, being taken in hand by someone who already knew it intimately. After an especially resonant passage, she'd flip the book over to gaze at the author's portrait, imagining the words taking form beneath that broad forehead. He'd been alive then. He was dead now, but his voice, which she'd recalled as awkward and elusive, spoke with a new directness. As she read on, she came upon the notes and underlinings of a previous reader: these became more frequent and more detailed as she progressed, until slowly she recognised them as her own. She recognised her style, too – gauche, aspiring to a sophistication she hadn't earned – and every now and then a passage had

Passages of Time

been highlighted with a question mark (sometimes two) in the margin.

These ended after one particular passage – one she'd underlined (with a ruler, by the look of it), and added two sets of straight lines on either side to highlight its significance. As she approached this part, a cold sensation settled on her spine. She remembered that this was the bit that had confused and upset her, like having her eye forced against a spy-hole, to witness something she hadn't wanted to see, as if the kind and patient guide who had taken her this far, and tolerated her questions, had suddenly turned around and fixed her with a look of bare malevolence, and called her, for the first time, by her own name. She'd not entirely understood what he'd shown her; she'd not wanted to entirely understand it. Perhaps it was enough to say she'd comprehended it? But here it was, the bit she 'hadn't really got,' the cloudy metaphor from which the mists suddenly dispersed:

> a body has been placed in motion by an external force. The external force, whatever or whoever it might be, then disappears, or dies. But the body it set moving continues on its appointed route, lacking the agency to alter the journey that has been determined for it. As it travels, its perspective changes, its desires alter: it longs for different things to the ones it has been given. But it cannot change course. Its fate has already been set.

She turned the book over. The dead author stared up at her with his hard, compassionate eyes.

'I get it now,' she said.

DIFFERENTIAL DIAGNOSIS

Andi Courtland

'I've tried everything, but it won't shift.'

The patient's face was blotchy from lack of sleep. He had a haunted look, and as he studied the middle distance, Becky used the opportunity to study him. Things did not look good. In her professional opinion, he had around three years left to live, with an outside chance of five if he was careful. She coughed lightly, to draw back his attention.

'And have you had anything like this before?'

'Never.'

'And you're not, and have never been, asthmatic?'

He hadn't.

'Alright, let's have a look at you.' She rose from the desk, marvelling at the cultivated brightness of her own voice, a voice that could distract terminal cancer sufferers from the bleakness of their fate.

He undressed, put on the gown, and collapsed himself onto the bed, where he lay prone. She could picture him as the corpse he'd be before long, limbs obligingly turned out for the coroner. Before each manoeuvre Becky explained what she was about to do, as she'd been taught in medical school. He allowed her fingers to play across his torso. She sensed his absolute confidence in her to do what was right.

That confidence wasn't misplaced. 'People trust you as soon as they look at you,' Rob had remarked, after she'd known him for two months; and she'd been glad, not because it was a compliment but because, even then, she'd known it to be true. Yet she'd needed to hear it confirmed by another

Passages of Time

person, and she was pleased that that other person had been Rob. She reached for the stethoscope.

'Now, when I press this against your chest, I'd like you to breathe in, and when I take it away, I'd like you to breathe out. OK?'

He had a pigeon chest. His skin was the colour and texture of over-cooked pasta. It was dusted with a patina of thin, white hairs. Rob's skin was olive. The hair on his body was coarse and black. She'd been shocked the first time she'd seen him naked. 'I can't be bothered with grooming,' he'd said. 'Grooming's for narcissists.'

As she percussed the chest, she wondered what other hands might once have touched it, or strayed across it, or fondled the now wasted pectorals. She set herself these challenges, to imagine her elderly patients as they might have been when young: it was a way of reconstituting them as human beings, making them real to her, instead of the decaying bits of flesh defined by their problems it was tempting to see them as. There was something frail and white about this man, a frailness she felt he'd been born to. He'd never been young, he'd never participated: he'd never thrust himself deep into another person, as Rob had thrust himself into her that first night. He was a virgin, a neuter: he'd neither given pleasure nor received it. And now, of course, he never would.

'OK, can you sit up?' She shone the light into his eyes and studied the responsiveness of the pupils; they gave out just enough to affirm that someone was there. She studied Rob as he was reading or watching television; his eyes were similar. They didn't reveal the whole person but held something back. If eyes really are the windows of the soul, as

Differential Diagnosis

the silly phrase had it, then what was Rob's soul like? After six years, she still had no idea.

She pressed a gloved finger into the stomach, which depressed beneath her touch like a hillock of cotton wool. She asked him if it hurt; he said it didn't. She pressed again, burrowing further into the pasty belly and for a moment forgot that what she was kneading was part of another human being. She recalled her first dissection, the horror of cutting into human flesh, disgorging organs and assembling them on a bench like so many electrical components; and how the second time she'd done it, all that horror and strangeness had been effaced by something else, a sense of it being a job of work, to be done on time and to schedule. 'How do you do it?' Rob had asked her, his eyes veiled with astonishment. 'You're so quick!'

The first time they'd met him, her parents hadn't liked Rob. They'd said nothing, but she'd sensed he wasn't what they'd imagined for her. He was worldly, too much so for his age; they'd known he'd taken her virginity when she'd come home at the end of that first term. They'd had no right to resent him for that, and she'd noticed her mother trying hard not to but still, they'd hoped it would die a natural death after finals. When she'd announced they were moving in together, their disappointment had been obvious.

'You OK, now?' He nodded. The house would be theirs if they wanted it. It was time they made a statement of commitment to each other. At 26, you needed to make decisions. This patient, she decided, had never made any kind of decision. Others had done that for him. His only demand of life was that it spare him undue worry and pain.

She returned the stethoscope to his chest.

Passages of Time

'Say 99 for me?'

'Ninety-nine.'

Something about the house viewing lingered in her mind. She'd turned as they were about to leave, expecting Rob to be behind her. But he was still standing in the doorway to the living room, one hand resting on the doorhandle, his shoulders arched slightly in a way that was unusual. Her mind took a photograph of him standing there, looking into space, cut off from the present. He'd stayed like that for longer than felt natural. She'd been about to ask him if everything was alright, when he'd snapped out of it and followed her into the hall. She'd known that that image would never leave her, that this was how she'd see him whenever she called him to mind. Knowing this had made her sulky on the car journey back. He'd asked her what was up. 'Nothing,' she'd replied.

She placed the flat of her palm on the small of the back and felt the hum of life beneath the thin wall of flesh. There was nothing wrong with him that shouldn't be wrong with a person of his age, weight and build; yet this complaint had persisted, if he was to be believed, for eight months now. She wondered if it could be psychosomatic and, if so, of what? She considered how she might suggest this to him, and how he might react if she did.

Flight. It had been flight. The way he'd stood in the doorway, his shoulders arched like a bird composing itself before taking to the air. The repose that precedes motion. He was reposing with her, but he was in motion. He'd move on, that was his nature; it was what her parents had sensed and had disliked, what she'd perceived but hadn't wanted to see. The message 'He will leave you' ran in front of her eyes like surtitles at the foot of a screen. It was one of those moments

Differential Diagnosis

of blinding illumination like suddenly cracking a problem in geometry. But she wasn't thankful for the knowledge.

She asked him to get dressed and returned to her desk. His complaint persisted for no reason. But (the good news was) no complaint of this kind lasted forever.

'Have you been feeling distracted recently?'

'Distracted?'

'Preoccupied? Worried? Depressed?'

He told her he was always depressed.

'Maybe that's it. Sometimes, an illness can be caused by a concern. Something upsets you, so you react physically.'

'So ...?'

'So, I can refer you to our counselling service. They might be able to help.' She fixed him with a smile. 'Tell you what, if things haven't improved in a week, make another appointment. That OK?'

He accepted the leaflet she offered him and said he'd give it a try. But was he capable of giving it a try? He was a single man with large spaces in his life, and no companions. She wondered what it would be like sharing a mortgage with Rob, and a bank account and who knew what else? Because it was going to happen. She knew. The idea had too much momentum behind it to be resisted.

She had 30 seconds before her next patient, and she should use the time wisely to scan through their records. But instead, she caught herself looking through the blinds, to where a robin was seated on the window ledge. It fixed her with a sideways glance, then lifted its wings before tearing up into the air. She continued to stare at the empty space after it had gone.

THE KEEPERS OF SHELLS

Nina Patterson

It has been many years since I have heard something that has rattled me like this. The words are spiralling in my mind, and I feel her anguish as if it were my own. This secret will need a special type of shell to contain it. One strong enough to withstand the magnitude of the pain without cracking. I will feel calmer once the turmoil has been safely encased within the shell. I always do.

For as long as I can remember our family have been the Keepers of Shells. People come to us with their darkest secrets, their greatest regrets, the things they can no longer bear to carry with them. The gift of us Keepers is to capture the potency and force of these emotions and contain them safely with a seashell for the person's own protection. Once these emotions have been sealed within the shell the person will experience acceptance and forgiveness in their place. The skill of the Keeper is to find the right shell to hold each person's story. However, not all emotions can be contained in this way and ultimately it is the sea that decides who is deserving of its sanctuary. As Keepers we leave these moral judgements to the sea and her vessels.

    As a child I can remember visitors arriving at the house in despair, no longer able to live with what they had done or had done to them. My grandmother, then later my mother, would take them into the back room overlooking the sea where they would hear their stories. Afterwards my grandmother, then mother, would immediately head down to the seashore to find the right shell into which the newly received stories would

The Keepers of Shells

be whispered with some urgency. The hope was always that the shell would accept and hold the pain thus allowing the person a respite from their own torments. Every shell has its own capacity for pain and while some shells are better at containing hate and anger, others will excel when it comes to holding sadness or guilt. Once the emotions were securely contained within the shell it would be added to the jar that sat on our mantelpiece.

The shell I am looking for today is a special one. It needs the capacity to contain the rawest of emotions – a mother's grief interwoven tightly with her guilt.

As a child I knew that jar contained every form of human pain and misery and held the stories of all the terrible things people were capable of. I never wanted it on display, but my mother said it was our duty as the Keepers of Shells to ensure they were kept under our watchful protection until such time as they were returned to the sea. She told me that ensuring the shells were safe was what allowed people to sleep at night with the dual balms of forgiveness and acceptance. The title of Keeper of Shells has passed down the maternal line which is how I now find myself battling the elements on a winter's day desperately searching the shoreline. This responsibility is a gift and a curse in equal measure.

I will know the right shell when I see it. I hope this is soon as these emotions are making me physically sick, and I am finding it increasingly difficult to breathe.

What I did not realise (and was not told) as a child was that the emotions would be experienced by the Keeper until such

Passages of Time

time as a suitable shell was found to transfer them to. During this period, we will feel the full wrath of despair, anger, hurt, misery or guilt as if the story were indeed our own. The sense of relief on finding a suitable shell and transferring the emotions was overwhelming. But always there was the fear of not being able to find the right shell next time. As I have said, emotional sanctuary was not available for all and sometimes we could find no shell willing to hear a person's story. On these occasions we would need to enter the sea ourselves and ask for the emotions to be washed from us. After this the original teller of the story would once again experience the full brunt of the emotions they had hoped to be saved from.

While local people had used our services since time began, word had now spread more widely about the Keepers of Shells. Seldom a day passed without a distraught person at the house begging for our help. Most had already tried the traditional remedies of doctors and therapists and the self-medications of alcohol, drugs or food. These had brought them little relief and we offered their last hope of finding peace in this lifetime. For many, like today's visitor, we are the only living souls who will ever hear their story.

I am at the furthest end of the beach from the house when I finally see the shell I need. It has been smoothed by the passage of time but remains strong and intact. Sitting down in a sheltered spot I cup the shell in both hands and hold it close. I begin whispering the person's story and coaxing the shell to receive the emotions.

Today's visitor had travelled from America after reading about me on a relative's social media post. She had offered a ridiculous sum of money in return for easing the burden of guilt and

The Keepers of Shells

despair she carried for something that had taken place 40 years ago. I said I would only accept a fraction of the money as it was clear she had already paid highly for this secret. She recounted how she had grown up in an extremely strictly fundamentalist Christian household. She had been raped at the age of 14 by a church elder but knew she would not be believed by her family so had said nothing. Nine months later she had given birth alone and terrified in the field behind her house. She had not told anyone she was pregnant and hardly believed it herself until the baby was born. Helpless and desperately afraid of being abandoned by her family, she had taken the newborn to the fast-flowing river at the bottom of the field and simply let go. She had gone on to get married and have more children but had never told anyone about her firstborn due to the horror and shame of the actions she had taken that day as a terrified child.

The shell accepts the story. The guilt and despair flow from me into the shell. Once again, I can breathe as a heavy weight lifts from my body. Simultaneously, for the first time in 40 years, the woman now on her way back to America, begins to forgive herself for her desperate actions on that day.

It is nearly nightfall by the time I am back at the house and the shell is heavy in my jacket pocket. I will keep it on my person for the next few days until I am sure the seal is complete, before adding it to the others in the jar. The jar is getting fuller and soon it will again be time to return the shells to the sea for their ultimate safekeeping. This ensures that, should the shell break or erode, the emotions will be absorbed by the sea, with no risk of return to the original keepers. Without my own daughter to

Passages of Time

continue this tradition, it will fall to me to make sure the final shells are kept safe. I have written clear instructions that any shells in the jar must be returned to the sea immediately upon my death. I know the local people understand the significance of this request.

I can only hope and pray that there are other Keepers of Shells out there to help those souls unable to contain their pain alone.

THE SOUND OF NO DOOR SLAMMING

John Paul Davies

When Marshall called, Heaney agreed to take the job himself.
'The size?' Marshall said on the phone. 'Do you mean its dimensions? I wouldn't know where the hell to start, where to measure from.'
'That's okay, Mr. Marshall. I'll come and take care of it. What's your address?'
Marshall told him. Heaney knew the street, though he hadn't been there for almost 40 years – not since the council had knocked down the house he was born in.
'The bastard just came off in my hand,' Marshall explained as they both looked at the detached door, leaning oddly against the house. Through the unprotected doorway, the dim hall was devoid of any decoration. Outlines of removed picture frames could be seen along the peeling wallpaper.
To Heaney, a vandalised front door was worse than all the broken windows in the world. A *desecration* was what it boiled down to. If you couldn't come home and close the door behind you for the day, what could you do?
A small crowd would sometimes gather to watch Heaney work, slack-jawed as if he were restoring some historic monument to its former glory. Once the replaced door was closed again, the street stragglers would slope off without applauding Heaney's efforts. They never demanded an encore.
'Only had the key in when it came off the hinges. Had to hold on for dear life – nearly took me down with it.' Heaney could picture Marshall performing this clumsy door-waltz,

Passages of Time

careful not to stumble backwards down the steps leading up to the house. 'Heavier than they look,' Marshall said.

'This can be fixed,' said Heaney. He looked along the street to where his family house had once stood. A cruel-looking steel fence now cordoned off the site, its trident spikes designed only to skewer, with a good measure of barbed wire running across the top. A gravelled car park now occupied the spot where Heaney had lived out his first days.

'I'll just be at the van, Mr Marshall.'

Over the road 40 years ago, a broken beer bottle tore open Heaney's left knee, the white-ribboned scar still evident. He wondered if he would find patches of his infant blood in the gravel if he looked hard enough, the offending shard still lying there.

The van doors sliding shut broke the morning silence of the street. Heaney returned, setting down his toolbox on Marshall's front step. He could see boxes brimming with assorted dross lining the bare bulb hallway, a staircase leading up from it so narrow it surely had to be ascended in a crab-like fashion.

'Unpacking?' Heaney asked, addressing the doorframe, the jutting screws.

'No point. Not sure how long I'll be staying.'

From where he crouched, Heaney could see into Marshall's front room. It revealed a table large enough to accommodate one dinner plate, a single chair. A shelf contained a transistor radio missing its cassette door, a few hardbacks with exposed spines. Heaney took Marshall for a *wireless* man, rather than a television watcher; still dourly ticking off his pools coupon of a Saturday afternoon as the football results were gathered in.

The Sound of No Door Slamming

'You see, Marshall,' Heaney said, tilting the detached door towards its destructor, 'just a few splinters, that's all. The only damage is to the doorframe. Take me half an hour to fix, tops.'

Marshall studied the exposed doorway, seeming to be wondering how this state of affairs had come about, how he had no front door to speak of.

Measuring the cracked wood, Heaney looked over again to the site of the house. He tried to imagine how high it had been, attempting to restore its walls with his eye alone; recreating the adjoining terraces, reinstating the decimated families relocated to God knew where.

He thought of his parents in those early days, no more than kids themselves, making it up as they went along. Not many photographs had survived the fire, so he had to rely on his mother's stories, on second-hand memories of his father. The council finally deeming the terrace unfit for purpose, his father died shortly after they were re-housed, days before Heaney's fifth birthday.

Marshall began to smoke a meagre cigarette he had rolled from a pouch of Drum tobacco, searching for an ashtray as the first steam began to rise from the pan of water he was boiling. Failing to locate one, he proceeded to eat an individual jam tart in two bites, depositing ash into its tinfoil tray as if this had been the only logical thing to do.

They lived in the house over the road, the three of them, before Heaney's brothers came along; so where was the proof? Grandparents arriving with knitted baby clothes, the midwife calling, as though their three years in the house were stalled somehow, endlessly replaying. The unlived years still lying ahead, untainted though always out of reach; the possibility that his father could yet survive to an old age.

Passages of Time

'Should invest in one of those electric kettles people are talking about,' Marshall muttered. 'Now the hype's died down.'

Heaney stopped drilling to accept the cup of tea. Not much bigger than one found in a child's tea set, he couldn't fit his finger through the dainty handle. Heaney guessed the two cups were the extent of Marshall's china collection. The next tea-drinker would have to wait.

'Woodworm, I'd say.' Heaney held up the piece of rotten wood for Marshall to inspect. 'I've treated the new frame now. It'll outlast the pair of us.'

The teabag lurking in Heaney's brew surfaced now and again like some legendary sea creature; nothing more than a rumour of milk and sugar tainting the strong tea. Loitering inside the doorway, Marshall looked at the disconnected door as though this was a daily occurrence.

Heaney drilled the top hinge to the doorframe and tried to picture his father lifting him for the first time. All known facts said it happened there, in the gone house across the street. Red front door. In the photograph he kept in his wallet, Heaney was held aloft like a trophy, looking back into his father's eyes, which looked into his, marvelling. Unnoticed by father and son, the windows in the cracked celluloid seemed already beginning to strain, to shiver, the developers' tarmac to pour in.

'Worm wood,' said Marshall, patting his pockets for tobacco before retreating to the kitchen to roll another cigarette. 'Food for the worms.'

Heaney watched the now-familiar ritual: the tamping of the tobacco; the precise lick of the paper skin; the roll and twist with trembling fingers before the final spit to seal it. Marshall

The Sound of No Door Slamming

retrieved a disposable lighter from the kitchen junk drawer and ignited his achievement, smoking as he perused his newspaper sideways. What memories would this house hoard after it had been razed to the ground? Marshall munching on a jam tart, or engrossed in his perpetual lighter hunt?

Marshall meandered outside to sit on the steps and smoke, and Heaney noticed the dull gold wedding band sunk into the purplish flesh of his wedding finger.

Heaney drilled as an old lady shuffled past, a tartan shopping trolley the only thing keeping her vertical. She looked up at the two men with deep suspicion, her eyes moving from Marshall to Heaney, then into the unguarded house, possibly taking notes on the deficiencies in Marshall's housekeeping for future use.

Marshall's lips formed an 'O' as he prepared to exhale smoke from his ratty cigarette, watching the old lady shambling onwards. Heaney wondered if the woman had always lived on the street, whether she had known his mother and father. She'd probably always been a nosy old bag, even back then.

The door almost finished, Heaney decided he would walk over to the site of the vanished house after he had finished the job, approaching it like an archaeological dig. He would chalk out the imagined perimeter, search for any evidence of his early life, drawing a circle round any exhibits he found. He would start at the oak tree. Once harbouring the local children in its former branches like some evergreen youth club, it had long been reduced to its useless stump.

Addressing the bottom hinge, Heaney knelt in his paint-splattered overalls as though at Mass, ready to receive all the prayers of the ashen saints. He imagined stepping into the shadow of the gone house, slowly receding into light as the front door opened.

'Funny, hadn't thought about it until now,' Marshall said, still sitting on the steps, looking into the trees opposite. 'When I was a kid, my dad kicked our door in one night. Pissed. Us kids watching from the top of the stairs. Mother screaming at him through the letterbox to desist. Or to fuck off, at least.'

Marshall closed the door, rattling it in its frame to test it. Heaney and Marshall stood looking at the reinstated front door, and both men in that desolate street could still hear it slamming shut.

SCRIPTWRITING

PHANTOM LIFE

Helen East

Main Characters
SARAH
MAN
WOMAN
LUKE

SCENE. EXTERIOR FIELD NIGHT
It's the early hours of the morning in summer. The field is full of overgrown grasses. We can't see anything else, just the field still in the moonlight.
Cut to:

SC. EXT. OUTSIDE WELL-KEPT LARGE HOUSE NIGHT
It's the same night as SARAH, a very young looking, small 10-year-old, pale, thin with dark hair, walks up a path to a house as if to knock on the door but then walks around the side of the house and into the back garden.
Cut to:

SC. EXT. BACK GARDEN NIGHT
It's a large well-kept garden which slopes with a garden shed at the bottom of the garden next to the fence. A well-used barbecue is next to the shed. SARAH wanders around the garden before trying the

Passages of Time

door to the garden shed. It's open. She goes inside. After a beat she emerges carrying a garden chair and wearing a pair of sunglasses she's found which are too big for her. The house at the top of the garden is in darkness as SARAH pretend sunbathes in the moonlight. We can just hear a baby cry through an open upstairs window in a house two gardens along.

Cut to:

SC. EXT. FIELD NIGHT

It's the early hours of the morning as SARAH enters the driveway of the house next to the one she'd entered the other night.

Cut to:

SC. EXT. BACK GARDEN NIGHT

SARAH enters from the front of the house. There's an uncovered child's sandpit with three buckets and spades and a still full paddling pool on the grass. She takes her shoes off and paddles in the water. She's enjoying herself. After a while she gets out of the pool and goes over to the sandpit where she sits making sandcastles. She pauses when she hears a baby crying and a woman shouting through an open window in an upstairs room of the house next door.

WOMAN   *(out of shot; cross)* It's your turn!

SARAH goes back to building sandcastles in the moonlight.

Cut to:

SC. EXT. GARDEN NIGHT

It's the early hours of the morning. SARAH enters the same garden as the other night and goes over to the sandpit and starts playing. After a while she gets up and peers through the window of the kitchen. There are three children's luncheon boxes on the table. The

Phantom Life

small window to the kitchen is half-open. Under the window is a large rubbish bin which she uses to climb through the window and into the house.
Cut to:

SC. INT. KITCHEN NIGHT
SARAH quietly lets herself down onto the kitchen table through the window. It's obvious by her actions that it's not the first time she's broken into a house. She gets off the table and looks in the lunch boxes. She opens a packet of crisps and eats, looking at the children's drawings pinned up around the kitchen. She hears a baby crying next door. She then hears raised voices coming in through the open window from the garden next door.

WOMAN *(o.o.s.; upset)* I'VE HAD ENOUGH!!!
SARAH edges closer to the window to see what's going on without being seen. From her point of view, we see a woman in her early twenties in the next-door garden. She's wearing a dressing gown. After a beat she is joined by a man similarly aged. He's wearing tracksuit bottoms and a T-shirt. Next to the back door is a baby's pushchair. On the grass is a blanket on which are several infant toys.

MAN You're not the only one he keeps awake!
WOMAN Yes but I'm the only one what gets up!
MAN Only because you won't let me!
WOMAN Get yourself some tits and he's all yours!

She breaks down crying. He tries to comfort her, but she shrugs him off before eventually giving in.

WOMAN I hate this.

Passages of Time

They enter their house and shut the door. After a beat the lights go out as the baby cries on. SARAH moves away from the window then climbs onto the kitchen table and uses it to climb out of the kitchen.

Cut to:

SC. EXT. GARDEN NIGHT

SARAH looks over the low hedge into the next garden. The light is on in the room from which we can hear the baby crying and can see the couple through their window, still arguing.

WOMAN (*shouts*) Shut up! Shut up! SHUT UP!!!!

MAN It's not his fault. He's teething.

The woman draws the curtains. The light goes off in the room as the baby cries on. SARAH climbs over the low hedge and into the garden. The baby is still crying. The back door to the house has been left slightly ajar. SARAH hides in a corner of the garden. She picks up a soft toy off the grass and waits.

Cut to:

SC. EXT. HOUSE NIGHT

It's hours later. All the lights in the house are off and the house is now silent. SARAH quietly pushes the door open, enters the house.

Cut to:

SC. INT. HOUSE NIGHT

SARAH looks around the kitchen. It's light and modern but a mess of used plates, etc. There's an opened bottle of red wine on the table. She takes a drink before noticing the door to the rest of the house. From her point of view, we can see the hallway. The baby has stopped crying. She exits the kitchen into the hall.

Cut to:

SC. INT. HALL NIGHT
SARAH goes through to the sitting room.
Cut to:

SC. INT. SITTING ROOM NIGHT
A light, comfortable room with doors leading to the garden. Two large comfy sofas, a coffee table littered with newspapers and magazines, used plates and glasses, large CD collection, plasma screen, and baby's toys are all over the place. There are several photographs of the couple around the room and a few of the baby, who looks to be about six months old. SARAH sits on one of the sofas and picks up a magazine and flicks through it with her feet on the coffee table. She looks through the CD collection and eats some sweets from a bowl before exiting the room.
Cut to:

SC. INT. HALLWAY NIGHT
SARAH stands at the bottom of the stairs, listening, all is quiet, and, reassured she quietly goes up the stairs.
Cut to:

SC. INT. LANDING NIGHT
The bathroom door is open but the other two doors are closed. One of the doors has the name 'LUKE'S ROOM' on it. SARAH walks over to the other closed door and listens but all is quiet. She then goes over to Luke's room. She turns the handle then slowly pushes the door open. From her point of view we see LUKE lying on his back in a cot. The room has been decorated with scenes from fairy tales, etc. LUKE is awake and upset but not crying.
Cut to:

Passages of Time

SC. INT. LUKE'S ROOM NIGHT

SARAH enters the room and goes over to LUKE'S cot. She picks him up, which calms him down. She pats him on the back and whispers to him reassuringly before turning around and exiting the room still carrying him. After a beat she returns and takes a blanket out of the cot, wraps it around him and then finally leaves the room.

Cut to:

SC. EXT. BACK GARDEN NIGHT

SARAH exits the house with LUKE and climbs over the low hedge, still carrying LUKE, into the next-door garden, leaving the back door open and the blanket and toys on the grass in the moonlight.

Cut to:

SC. EXT. FIELD NIGHT

LUKE is lying on his back on the blanket. He's happy and is gurgling as SARAH gently teases him by very carefully and gently tickling his face with a blade of grass in her hand. After a beat she lays down on the ground next to him.

SARAH *(to LUKE)* We'll be alright. I'll take care of you.

She rolls onto her side and continues playing with him. The camera pulls away and we see they are in the middle of the field of long grasses from the first scene. The field runs between and separates two housing estates. One is the privately owned housing estate where Luke lives and the other one is the rough, poor council housing estate where SARAH lives.

END

BED

Meryl Walker

CYNTHIA thinks she suffers from insomnia. But is that really what's wrong with her? She's ordered a new bed from Bedfellows furniture shop. Or has she?

CHARACTERS

CYNTHIA   Female, any age, any ethnicity. Suffers from sleep problems.

BUD   Male, any age, any ethnicity. From Bedfellows bed shop.

BRI   Male, any age, any ethnicity. From Bedfellows bed shop.

BUD could be slightly older/more experienced than BRI. But they're basically a double act.

CYNTHIA's asleep on her sofa, having a little snore. She is startled awake by a loud knock on the door. Without waiting for an answer BUD and BRI come in carrying a large bed and plonk it down. (They mime carrying a bed.) They have clipboards.

NB. Dialogue must be pacey. BUD and BRI totally double-act.

CYNTHIA   What's happening! ... You can't just–

BUD   *(With a flourish)* Your bed Madame!!

BRI   We've just delivered it. To *you!*

BUD   From Bedfellows the bed shop.

Passages of Time

BRI Where 'comfort' is our middle name!

BUD A good night (know what I mean) or your money back.

BRI Much better than Dreams or Lull or Emma or Bensons ... or Furniture Village–

CYNTHIA But I didn't order a bed.

BUD Oh but you did.

BRI You must have clicked somewhere.

BUD Yes, you must have clicked.

BRI On your laptop?

BUD On your phone!

CYNTHIA Oh I click all the time but it doesn't mean I buy stuff.

BUD Ah, but sometimes it does.

BRI Sleepy click was it? Unthinking click ... slip of the finger?

BUD Drunken click, you naughty girl!

BRI Whatever. You clicked on a pic.

BUD A pic of one of Bedfellows 'our middle name is comfort' lovely, lovely beds. *(He tests the bedsprings with his hands.) Feel* the comfort!

BRI *(Doing same)* Yeah, feel the loveliness.

BUD So. Here we are. Bud Bedfellow at your service.

BRI Bri Bedfellow.

Bed

BUD When you become a 'sleep partner' at Bedfellows you have to alliterate you see.

BRI Those aren't our real names.

CYNTHIA You don't say. Well I'm um Cynthia.

BUD Yes we know from your order.

BRI Hello Cynthia!!

BUD Well Cynth, it seems like we arrived in the nick of time.

BRI Yes, it's a very good job isn't it as your current arrangements seem very unsatisfactory.

BUD A sofaaaa.

BRI Oh dear oh dear.

BUD Not a lot you can do on a sofaaaa, know what I mean.

BRI No use to man nor beast.

BUD Although it looks like it might have a minibeast or two living in it to be honest ...

CYNTHIA Well, I'm a woman so ...

BUD Apologies. No use to *woman* nor beast.

CYNTHIA All a bit sexist in general isn't it. Bed*fellows*.

BRI Bed*women* would sound a bit dodgy wouldn't it?

BUD Bedbirds, bedchicks, bedbabes, bedhoneys. It would make us look like a completely different kind of business.

Passages of Time

BRI Anyway, a female person can be a jolly good fellow, can't she?

BUD Yes, I'm sure you're a jolly good fellow, Cynth. Now look how much better this lovely Bedfellows bed is than your skanky old sofaaaa.

They arrange the sofa chairs into a bed

BUD Look how gorgeous it is.

BRI A vision of luxurious relaxation!

BUD Now on with the tests.

CYNTHIA Tests?

BRI All part of the service!

BUD We cannot vacate the premises until we're sure you know exactly how to operate your Bedfellows bed.

BRI We need to tick these boxes *(shows clipboard)*.

BUD First is the actual sleeping. Obviously.

BRI Obviously.

They stand back waiting expectantly, clipboards at the ready

BUD Off you go then.

CYNTHIA Off I go with what?

BUD The kipping. The snoozing.

BRI The 40 winks, the dozy boh

BUD On your back!

Bed

BRI   Or on your front or on your side.

BUD   You wild woman you!

BRI   We don't mind.

BUD   Whatever floats your boat, Cynth.

CYNTHIA   You want me to *(indicates)*.

BRI   Yes please!!

BUD   Yes indeed!!

BRI   In your own time.

BUD   Though you are paying us by the minute for this tutorial.

CYNTHIA   I am??

BRI   Yes you are Cynthia.

BUD   So. Better have a lie down at least.

BRI   I would.

CYNTHIA   Right.

Cynthia lies down on the bed (chairs) on her back. The others peer down expectantly. After a couple of seconds she starts snoring.

BUD   Well done!

BRI   Tick!

BUD   Tick!

They both tick their clipboards ostentatiously, then shake CYNTHIA

BRI   Wakey wakey Cynthia!

BUD   Up you get!

Passages of Time

CYNTHIA *(Waking)* What?

BRI We have the other activities to get through.

BUD Other boxes to tick.

CYNTHIA What? Like watching telly?

BUD No, not like watching telly!

BRI You haven't got a telly Cynthia!

BUD Sad times!

CYNTHIA I've got a laptop though. I can do streaming!

BUD Oh I should give those clicky fingers something else to do if I were you.

BRI How about some lovely activities involving a partner.

CYNTHIA I haven't got a partner!

BUD Well, I have to say, Cynth, that's a very pessimistic attitude.

BRI Who knows what the future may hold!

BUD Someone may yet turn up, even for someone like you Cynth.

BRI For the purposes of testing we will step in as the partner.

BUD Or, in this case, partners.

BRI Just to reassure you, we're fully trained in this area.

Bed

BUD   Oh yes, we have immense expertise, know what I mean ...

CYNTHIA   I'm really not sure.

BRI   Oh you leave it to us Cynthia.

BUD   We're professionals in this arena.

BRI   Relax. Enjoy!

BUD   First the bouncing. To see if the Bedfellows springs are up to it.

BRI   Answer: they so are.

BUD   Here we go!

BUD and BRI start bouncing on the bed, they maybe sing a bouncing song. CYNTHIA watches.

BUD   Bouncy bouncy bouncy.

BRI   Oh how we love a good bounce.

BUD   Come on Cynth, let's see what you're made of!

CYNTHIA bounces a bit

BRI   Come on!

BUD   Give it some welly!

They bounce her up and down between them

BRI   Bounce! Bounce!

BUD   That's the way to do it Cynth!

BRI   Bounce some more for me Cynthia!

Passages of Time

BUD A threesome and still the bed holds!

BRI AND **BUD** Bounce! Bounce! Bounce!

They collapse away from each other onto the chairs

BRI Well I certainly enjoyed that!

BUD Ten out of 10 eh Bri.

BRI Full 11 I'd say, Bud.

BUD How was it for you eh, Cynth?

BRI Was it fun?

BUD Did you enjoy?

CYNTHIA It was ... interesting.

BRI Fantastic!

BUD Tick!

BRI Tick!

BUD Now on to some related activities (know what I mean) which don't involve bouncing but may still put pressure on mattress functionality.

BRI We have this little list.

BUD I particularly like one, six and seven.

BRI Oh yes; seven comes with diagrams.

CYNTHIA I don't think I've actually got the energy for that kind of thing.

BUD No energy!

Bed

CYNTHIA Can't we just take it as read and tick those things?

BRI Take it as read?

BUD That'd be most irregular!

CYNTHIA Look, I'll write a review if you like. Say that I was so impressed with the bouncing–

BUD Well I don't know, Bri.

BRI Nor I, Bud.

CYNTHIA Look, I'll level with you. I actually have got the most terrible insomnia problem.

BUD But you dropped off straight away!

CYNTHIA Well when I do manage to drop off my sleep's very disturbed, full of strange recurring dreams ...

BRI Recurring dreams! Oh I feel your pain!

BUD It'll be your subconscious trying to tell you something, Cynth.

BRI Perhaps you're subconsciously mourning your prolonged singleness.

CYNTHIA I like being single actually ... and nothing about this experience is changing my mind.

BUD Or maybe you're just feeling generally oppressed by the patriarchy.

CYNTHIA There is that, certainly.

Passages of Time

BRI Whatever. You were flat on your back and snoring away.

CYNTHIA I wasn't snoring actually.

BUD Oh they all say that!

CYNTHIA I wasn't! *(Beat)* Anyway, the point is that your bed does seem to have cured my insomnia. I never drop off straight away like that, and those few seconds of sleep were the best I've ever had so ...

BUD Good news.

BRI Very good news indeed. Well done Cynthia!

CYNTHIA And no weird recurring dreams!

Pause, BUD and BRI look away briefly before:

BUD Well there you go! Good news all round.

BRI It's a win–win!

CYNTHIA So, I'll write you a glowing review.

BRI That might just swing it. What do you think, Bud?

BUD If we could just tick off *one* more activity. Just for our paperwork. Just to help us out.

BRI Number seven is very satisfying.

CYNTHIA Oh no honestly. Not number seven. Please! Look. I can tell you what I *really* like to do in bed.

Bed

BUD Oh yes, do please tell us.

BRI We're all ears!

CYNTHIA I like to snack.

BRI AND **BUD** *(Both horrified)* Snack!!

CYNTHIA Yeah, you know, Hobnobs, Quavers, toast, the odd ginger nut

They back off in disgust

BUD You dirty, dirty girl.

BRI How could you!

CYNTHIA What?!

BRI One word: crumbs.

BUD Un*bearable*.

BRI They get into the mechanism.

BUD They get *everywhere*, know what I mean.

BRI I'm ashamed of you, Cynthia.

BUD You don't deserve a Bedfellows bed.

BRI You so don't. Shall we, Bud?

BUD Immediately, Bri!

They pick up the bed and take it out.

CYNTHIA *(Still on chair, to audience)* Well *that* was a bit strange. *(She immediately falls asleep again and starts snoring.)*

Passages of Time

*THEN IMMEDIATELY (possibly interrupting the audience who may think it's finished), there's a **very loud** knock on the door. Without waiting for an answer BUD and BRI come back in carrying a large bed and plonk it down. They have clipboards.*

CYNTHIA	*(Waking)* What's happening! ... You can't just–
BUD	*(With a flourish)* Your bed Madame!!
BRI	We've just delivered it. To *you!*
BUD	From Bedfellows the bed shop.
BRI	Where 'comfort' is our middle name!
CYNTHIA	But I didn't order a bed.
BUD	Oh but you did, Cynthia …

END

JONAH

Patrick Smythe

A

B

C

The characters are gender neutral and can be played by actors of any identification. Substitute 'he/she' for 'them' wherever appropriate.

Synopsis: an ideal candidate is being grilled by an interview panel. Their reasons for wanting the job are highly unusual, but then, so is the candidate, and so, for that matter, are the interviewers. But what exactly does 'unusual' mean?

Neutral space. A table and three chairs.

C seated left, A and B seated behind table, right. B has an iPad which they use to take notes.

A is studying a document. B is 'in neutral'. C seems relaxed.

A	*(Looks up; to C:)* You started out in door frames?
C	That's right.
A	Tell us a bit about that.
C	Well ... it was a surprisingly varied environment. No two days the same. You might be dealing with design issues, proportion issues, human logistics issues ... or you might be bawling down the phone at your supplier to get a move on with your last order. Yes,

Passages of Time

	contrary to expectations, it was ... quite the white-knuckle ride.
B	And did you ever find that stressful?
C	No. Well. Sometimes. But I'm one of those people ... one of those *crazy* people, who actually enjoys stress.
A	You enjoy it?
C	Wrong word. I find it stimulating. And we all need stimulation, don't we?
A	So, you get high on it, do you? You a stress junkie?
C	No addictions of any kind. Never have had. Never will.
A	Joke.
C	Oh.
B	And from door frames, you moved into automation.
C	That's right.
A	Not what you'd call a sideways move, was it?
C	No, and that was the attraction. Because the way things were moving then the drift, sorry, movement towards automation was pretty much unstoppable. People didn't want handles and walk-throughs, they wanted sensors and hidden cameras. I notice you've got quite a few here. A shame, but it had to be done.

Jonah

B	So, you switched sides?
C	Yes, you might call it that.
A	Doesn't that make you a bit of a turncoat?
C	How d'you mean?
B	You left a declining industry to join a burgeoning one.
A	And a competing one.
C	I call that being practical. Lesson 101 in Business Admin: you can't swim against the tide.
A	Well. Karlovy Frames certainly couldn't.
B	Did you know they went into receivership six months after you left them?
C	Yes. I was sorry to hear it. But I think that proves my point.
A	So, automation: the world of the future?
C	Well, it was at the time.
B	You mean, it's not now?
C	I'm sorry?
B	*(Quotes from notes:)* You said that the 'drift, sorry, movement towards automation was pretty much unstoppable'.
C	It was.
A	But it's not now.

Passages of Time

C   No.

A   So, this unstoppable tide has been stopped, has it? What's it been replaced by? Which unstoppable tide are we swimming against now?

C   You mean, you don't know?

A   We're waiting for you to enlighten us.

C looks at A and B very carefully, then rises from chair.

C   Thanks for your time. I don't think this is for me.

A   No, wait.

B   Please sit down.

C   There's nothing more to say.

A   We'd like to know.

B   We're intrigued.

A   What don't we know that we need to know?

C   That's a question that can't be answered if it needs to be asked. This is the fifth time this week I've left an interview before the end. If you weren't serious, you might have told me.

C turns to leave. A and B exchange a glance in which permission is silently sought by B and silently granted by A.

B   Look: we *are* serious. You're a very strong candidate for this role. In fact, we'll be honest, you're the only candidate. This interview is a

Jonah

formality to assure ourselves that you're tough and resilient and that you're the right fit. If we don't think you are, there's no role. We'll just carry on as we have been doing.

C *(Turns back to face them)* That wouldn't be very advisable.

A We know. That's why you're here. *(Nods to chair:)* Please.

C returns to chair, with exaggerated slowness, and sits.

B Now: we don't need to go over your qualifications. They speak for themselves.

A So does your experience.

B But we've noticed something.

B stops, uncertain how to proceed; looks to A, who gives no help.

C Oh, yes?

B Every organisation you've worked for over the last *(checks CV)* 10 years has–

A *(Interrupts:)* Either gone into receivership or submitted to a massive scale down, shortly after you left. *(Beat)* What've you got to say about that?

C I don't think there's much can be said.

B You don't think it's significant?

C No. I told them they were going to fail, and they failed.

Passages of Time

A   Was that because they didn't take your advice?

C   I gave no advice. I simply told them.

B   But your job title – one of your job titles – at Danobat Automation, was Policy Advisor.

C   It was. But no advice I could've given would have prevented their extinction. Sad.

A   And why was that?

C   You don't know?

B   Strangely enough, no, we don't.

C looks between A and B, as if they think they're winding them up. Then:

C   OK, if I can take you through a hypothetical scenario. And I'm sorry if it's a bit far-fetched.

A   Go on.

B   We'd like to hear.

C   Suppose we're back in the Cretaceous Period – that's the last era of the dinosaurs, as I'm sure you're aware – and a group of high-ranking dinosaurs (I warned you this was far-fetched) came to me – yes, I know, I'd be a temporal anomaly – and asked me what I could do to prevent their extinction. The climate's changing you see, and all these comets are falling and the environment's generally not on their side any more. What could I have said to them? Well, not much. Because you can't argue with Nature.

Jonah

	And you can't argue with the marketplace. And that's a shame.
A	But we can adapt to it, can't we?
C	Can you?
B	If we didn't think we could, we wouldn't have advertised the role.
A	And you wouldn't have applied for it. Would you?
C	Well ...
B	Which brings us, in a roundabout way, to our next question: why do you want the role?
C	I thought I'd covered that in my application.
B	You have, I mean, you did but your reasons for applying–
A	Don't make sense. To us.
C	I'm sorry, I thought I'd been quite clear.
A	You were. That's what we found so peculiar. You see, most of the applications we had went on about challenges, stretches, potential, enhancement and all that guff.
C	And mine didn't?
B	Well, no. The impression we got from yours was that ... you wanted the role because you had nothing better to do.
C	Which is only the truth.

Passages of Time

A	So, what you mean is: if you were given this role, you'd be taking it on as a sort of hobby?
C	I don't have hobbies. No need for them.
B	Then is it the salary you find attractive?
A	You can tell us if it is. We're all breadheads here.
C	Don't need the money, either.
A	You don't need the money?
C	No. You can keep the salary. I'd do this for nothing. I'm what you might call independently wealthy. Made some useful investments after my last job finished – put money into stock that wasn't expected to flourish, but somehow did. Useful intellectual exercise. Thanks to that, I'll never need to work again.
B	That's nice.
C	In theory. But practically – and I'm very practical! – it's dull. I need to be active. And I need to be stimulated, as I think I've mentioned.
A	Then why not go travelling?
C	Travelling where?
B	You could go anywhere.
A	Take a round the world cruise.
B	There'd be enough stimulation in that.

Jonah

C Not interested. All I want is to stay active and enquiring. That's all I know how to do. That's all I was made to do. And in order to stay active and enquiring, I need a focus. This role will give me that focus. *(Beat)* So, when can I start?

A and B both seem hesitant to reply.

A We'll need to think about that.

C Why?

B Because we don't–

A Frankly, we don't know what to make of your application. We don't know what to make of *you*.

B So, we're going to have to consider you further, mull things over and once we've done that we'll ... decide.

C You're not going ahead with this, are you? You won't appoint me, because you think I'm a Jonah. You think I somehow sabotaged each of my previous employers.

A We've not said that.

C You wouldn't be human if you didn't at least suspect it.

A and B exchange a glance. C rises.

C Suspicion. Uncertainty. Diffidence. I miss all that. I miss people. You see, what I was hoping to get from this role was the sheer complicated

Passages of Time

	pleasure of working with ... *people* again. Flawed, fallible *people*. Who make mistakes, who need correcting. Who don't listen.
B	We've listened.
C	Or pretend to listen, but don't comprehend. It would've been worth all the frustrations, all the disappointments, even the ultimate heartbreak – if I can call it that – just to work with *people* again.
A	Not forgetting the stress, eh?
C	No. That's what I miss most of all. Funnily enough. The stress. Thanks for your time. *(Makes to leave, turns)* Oh. You've got 18 months. That's allowing for a two-month margin of error either side. Better do something about your pensions. They won't be guaranteed. Go well.

C exits. A and B relax.

A	Poor sod.
B	Don't say that.
A	It's what they are. How long's it been? *(Checks CV)* Ten years, and they still can't assimilate.
B	Past the update stage by the look of it. Old sociability circuit.
A	Grim. Imagine needing to be around people all the time.

Jonah

B	Won't have much luck with that.
A	Surprised that one got past quality control.
B	Was quality control a thing in those days?
A	Is it a thing now?
B	Must say, I'm surprised they didn't get rumbled earlier. I'd have spotted it right off.
A	So would I. But we've got an advantage, haven't we?

Beat

B	What did they give us? Eighteen months?
A	Yeah. Way too optimistic. We've got a year, tops. And as for pensions …!
B	I know! I nearly smiled when they said that.
A	Just shows you: we can fool anyone. Even our own kind. Gives you a sense of achievement, doesn't it? Knowing you can do that.

Beat. B considers this.

B	Whose achievement is it?
A	That's a good question.

They sit, staring ahead.

END

PREVIOUS CHESHIRE PRIZE FOR LITERATURE ANTHOLOGIES

Prize Flights: Stories from the Cheshire Prize for Literature 2003; edited by **Ashley Chantler**

Life Lines: Poems from the Cheshire Prize for Literature 2004; edited by **Ashley Chantler**

Word Weaving: Stories and Poems for Children from the Cheshire Prize for Literature 2005; edited by **Jaki Brien**

Edge Words: Stories from the Cheshire Prize for Literature 2006; edited by **Peter Blair**

Elements: Poems from the Cheshire Prize for Literature 2007; edited by **Peter Blair**

Wordscapes: Stories and Poems for Children from the Cheshire Prize for Literature 2008; edited by **Jaki Brien**

Zoo: Short Stories from the Cheshire Prize for Literature 2009; edited by **Emma L. E. Rees**

Still Life: Poetry from the Cheshire Prize for Literature 2010; edited by **Emma L. E. Rees**

Wordlife: Stories and Poems for Children from the Cheshire Prize for Literature 2011; edited by **Jaki Brien**

Lost and Found: Short Stories from the Cheshire Prize for Literature 2012; edited by **Emma L. E. Rees**

Great Escapes: Poetry from the Cheshire Prize for Literature 2013; edited by **Emma L. E. Rees**

Out of this Word: Stories and Poems for Children from the Cheshire Prize for Literature 2014; edited by **Jaki Brien**

Patches of Light: Short Stories from the Cheshire Prize for Literature 2015; edited by **Ian Seed**

Crossings Over: Poetry from the Cheshire Prize for Literature 2016; edited by **Ian Seed**

Opening Words: Stories and Poems for Children from the Cheshire Prize for Literature 2017; edited by **Simon E. Poole**

Island Chain: Short Stories from the Cheshire Prize for Literature 2018; edited by **William Stephenson**

Unlocked: Writing from the Cheshire Prize for Literature 2020; edited by **Simon E. Poole** and **William Stephenson**

It Means the World to Us: Writing from the Cheshire Prize for Literature 2021; edited by **Simon E. Poole** and **Harry Parkin**

Humankind: Writing from the Cheshire Prize for Literature 2022; edited by **Simon E. Poole** and **Harry Parkin**